Sew Caroline

WEEKEND STYLE

15

Easy-Sew Patterns
for the Must-Have
Weekend Wardrobe

CAROLINE HULSE

Fons&Porter

D1473495

fw
a content + ecommerce company

www.fwcommunity.com

21 20 19 18 17   5 4 3 2 1

Distributed in Canada by Fraser Direct
100 Armstrong Avenue
Georgetown, ON, Canada L7G 5S4
Tel: (905) 877-4411

Distributed in the U.K. and Europe by F&W
MEDIA INTERNATIONAL
Pynes Hill Court, Pynes Hill, Rydon Lane
Exeter, EX2 5AZ, United Kingdom
Tel: (+44) 1392 797680
E-mail: enquiries@fwmedia.com

SRN: S9144
ISBN-13: 978-1-4402-4649-4

Editor: Maya Elson

Technical Editor: Debra Greenway

Designer: Alanna DiLiddo

Illustrator: Sue Friend and Caroline Hulse

Photographer: Sarah Delanie

CONTENTS

introduction

My sewing journey is not the typical sewn-all-my-life type of story. My mom sewed, but by the time I came around she had lost interest. My grandmothers didn't live nearby, and there was no one else offering to teach me. I spent the majority of my childhood outdoors riding my bike, playing in the sprinklers, and getting dirty. Creativity and fashion were the furthest things from my mind until midway through college. I was pursuing a business degree at Texas A&M when I found myself longing for a creative outlet. I tried drawing, painting, scrapbooking, etc., but nothing really stuck. And then I asked for a sewing machine for Christmas.

Since the sewing machine appeared under the tree in 2008, I have slowly and fiercely fallen in love with sewing. I am known in my family to jump into things without any knowledge or research, and this gift was no exception.

From the beginning, I fumbled my way through figuring out techniques by learning as I went. I watched approximately one million YouTube videos, read tons of blog articles, read many books, and went through a plethora of scrap fabric before I became proficient at threading my machine, dropping in the bobbin, and setting my tension correctly. If I had just taken a class or two, the learning process might have been faster, but I genuinely believe that the years I spent learning to love sewing on my own terms shaped me into the sewist I am today.

In a few short years, I went from DIY-style sewing to using patterns to designing my own patterns. The learning curve was steep, but the result was worth the effort—the garments I was eventually making and wearing felt more professional and legit. In 2014, I put my first pattern up for sale on my website (a simple knit dress called the Out and About Dress), and it has since sold thousands of copies and remains my top seller.

Through this journey, I have learned that there are many different ways to do things and that no one technique is always correct. With this as my basis, I am excited to share with you what I have learned over the years, different approaches to certain techniques, and encouragement to trust yourself to try new things, make mistakes, and work it out!

I wrote this book for women who love comfortable fashion and enjoy sewing their own clothing. It's designed to help make sewing your weekend wardrobe a breeze—and a joy. That's why I kept the patterns uncomplicated, instructions simple, and projects quick and satisfying to make.

I hope you love reading and sewing from this book as much as I loved writing it.

xoxo,
caroline

getting started

It may be tempting to jump right in and get started on all these fun Weekend Style projects, but before we do that, let's take a look at the tools we'll need to have a stress-free afternoon of sewing. It's important to have these items for when you need them. . . . Who has time to run to the store in the middle of a project?!

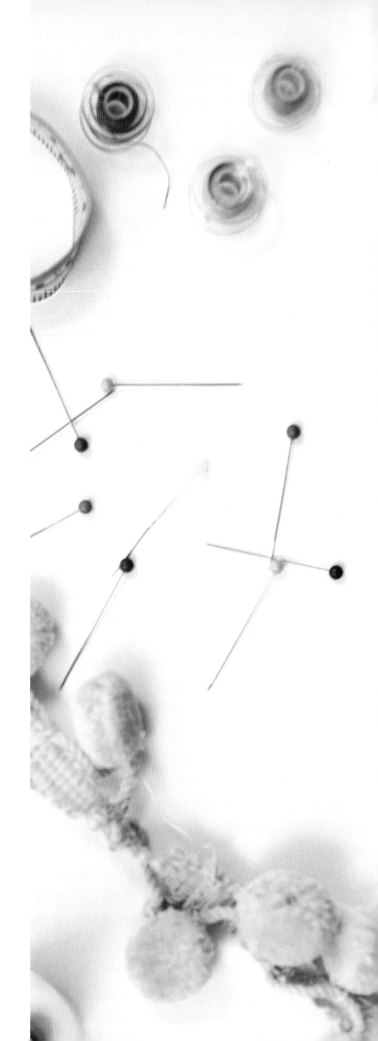

TOOLS OF THE TRADE

To make your sewing projects a little easier and less stressful, there are a few tools that you need to have on hand at all times. Here are my go-to tools for stress-free sewing (besides the obvious sewing machine):

DRESSMAKER'S SHEARS/ FABRIC SCISSORS

Go ahead and invest in a good (read: expensive) pair of fabric scissors. If taken care of properly, these can be used throughout your lifetime.

EMBROIDERY SCISSORS OR OTHER SMALL SCISSORS

You'll find yourself doing a lot of snipping while sewing; it's a good idea to have a smaller pair of "snips" on hand. I suggest grabbing ones that are easy to pick up and have super sharp blades.

PINS

Straight pins are a must for keeping fabric in its proper place while sewing. My favorites are the flower-head pins—just be sure to remove them before sewing!

MAGNETIC PINCUSHION

This is a great place to toss your pins so they don't get lost and scattered all over the floor.

SEAM RIPPER

Mistakes happen. And if you're anything like me, they happen often! Keeping a seam ripper (or two!) on hand at all times is insurance that your mistakes can be fixed.

EXTRA PRE-WOUND BOBBINS

There's honestly nothing sadder than finishing a long seam and realizing that halfway through it your bobbin thread ran out! How frustrating! Keeping already-wound bobbins on hand is a great way to ease the pain of an empty bobbin. Be sure you're using the correct bobbin for your machine; all machines take different ones.

NEUTRAL-COLORED THREAD

Most projects can be sewn with neutral-colored thread. My go-tos are gray and beige. I typically like to buy big spools of neutrals and smaller spools of color for topstitching.

MACHINE NEEDLES

Different types of machine needles are covered on page 19, but having extras on hand will save you the hassle of having to run to the store in the middle of a project.

MEASURING TAPE

A soft, flexible measuring tape is the perfect tool for taking measurements to determine the size pattern you need to sew. You'll also find yourself using a measuring tape throughout your project for various things.

BIAS TAPE MAKER

This nifty tool helps make creating bias tape a cinch! It comes in various sizes, including 6 mm, 12 mm, 18 mm, and 25 mm. For garments, I typically use the 18 mm maker, and that is the size I use in this book.

IRON AND IRONING BOARD

I *hate* ironing. When my husband asks me to iron his shirt, I give him a major eye roll. But pressing? Pressing is something I don't mind because I know it's going to allow my sewing project to look more professional and finished. Investing in a good iron and ironing board is a must for any serious stitcher—you'll be using it a lot! I like my iron to have a great steam setting, so keep that in mind when shopping. Be sure to check your heat settings with the type of fabric you're using. It would be a shame for your fabric to melt away!

ROTARY CUTTER AND MAT

Some people prefer using a rotary cutter and mat as opposed to fabric scissors. I say try them both and figure out what works best for you. If you're a quilter, you may already have a rotary cutter and mat on hand.

PATTERN WEIGHTS

Really, anything goes for pattern weights. A cell phone, a child's toy, a bottle of wine—basically anything that weighs more than paper. If you want to get fancy, you could consider purchasing actual pattern weights or large (3" [7.5 cm] or larger) washers.

MARKING TOOL

This item is really one of your preference, so choose a few and decide which you like best. Some options include tailor's chalk, disappearing ink pen, fabric pencil, tailor's wax, and tracing wheel.

CHOOSING
A FABRIC

In the beginning, the one thing that really attracted me to the idea of sewing was the fabric. I was enamored by the different styles, prints, colors, and textures that were present in all different types of textiles. Walking up and down the aisles of fabric stores touching everything I could, I looked at the way colors played with one another and studied the intricate designs. (Tell me I'm not the only one!) It was really confusing, however, when I'd look at the end of a bolt and see the "type" of fabric it was. I was a little clueless beyond soft, stretchy, velvety, etc. Here's a breakdown of common fabric types you'll see (and feel!) in fabric stores or listed on the back of patterns:

100% COTTON

A woven fabric that is suitable for many different uses such as garments and quilts. The "hand" or feel of a cotton fabric will differ depending on the quality of fibers used. A nice-quality cotton will be soft and supple to the touch. It may shrink during washing and drying.

LINEN

A breathable woven fabric used to make summertime shirts and pants. It wrinkles easily and will shrink during washing and drying.

VOILE

A lightweight, breathable cotton fabric that is soft to the touch and sews like butter. Use voile to sew a breezy top or a spring scarf.

RAYON

A breathable woven fabric with a silk-like "hand" or feel that drapes beautifully. Works best if sewn into a top or dress.

KNIT

A soft, breathable fabric that stretches when pulled. There are many different types of knits at various different percentages of stretch. Be sure you've chosen the right type of knit for your project. See page 17 to learn how to determine the stretch percentage of knit fabric and tips on choosing the right knit fabric for your project.

CANVAS

A midweight to heavyweight fabric that does not have great drape. It is best suited for more structured projects such as shorts or bags.

CHAMBRAY

A lightweight cotton fabric with a loose, breathable weave. Chambray is typically denim colored, but it does not have the same stiff, rigid properties of traditional denim. Use chambray to sew dresses, skirts, and tops.

TENCEL

A lot like rayon, Tencel is made from recycled wood pulp and has a wonderful "hand" or feel and drape. It does not wrinkle much and is great for sewing tops, dresses, and skirts.

TWILL

A midweight woven fabric that has structure. Twill can be sewn into shorts, pants, and some types of casual skirts.

CARING FOR YOUR FABRIC

	HOW TO WASH				HOW TO DRY		HOW TO IRON		PROJECT IDEAS
	Cold	Warm	Machine	Hand	Tumble	Lay flat/ Hang	Low	High	
Cotton	X	X	X		X			X	Bags, shorts, skirts
Linen	X	X	X		X			X	Pants, bags, hats
Voile	X	X	X		X	X		X	Dresses, tops
Rayon	X		X	X		X		X	Dresses, tops, skirts
Jersey Knit	X	X	X		X			X	Dresses, tops, skirts, casual wear, leggings
Canvas	X	X	X		X			X	Bags, skirts, shorts
Chambray	X	X	X		X			X	Skirts, tops
Tencel	X		X		X			X	Dresses, tops, skirts
Silk/Blends	X			X		X	X		Tops, skirts
Polyester/ Blends		X	X		X		X		Dresses, tops, skirts

DETERMINING STRETCH FOR KNIT FABRIC

It is important to know the stretch percentage of a knit fabric so you can determine how it is going to behave once sewn. Fabrics with greater stretch typically have a higher spandex content and greater stretch recovery (how a fabric "bounces back" after it has been stretched). For example, for the Tilly Tee pattern in this book, you'll want a knit that has at least a 40 percent stretch.

To determine stretch percentage, take a strip of fabric that is 4" (10 cm) wide (parallel to the selvedge) and about 8" (20.5 cm) across the width of the fabric. Fold it in half along the grainline (with the two selvedge edges touching). Place the folded edge of

the fabric at the zero mark on your ruler and hold it in place with your left hand. With your right hand, pull the fabric as far as it will stretch and note that distance. Once you've released your fabric, check the stretch recovery. Did your fabric go back to the 4" (10 cm) mark on the ruler, or did it stay somewhere around the 5" (12.5 cm) or 6" (15 cm) mark? If it went back to 4" (10 cm), your fabric has great stretch recovery. If it didn't, I'd stay away from that fabric, because once it is stretched it won't go back to its true form.

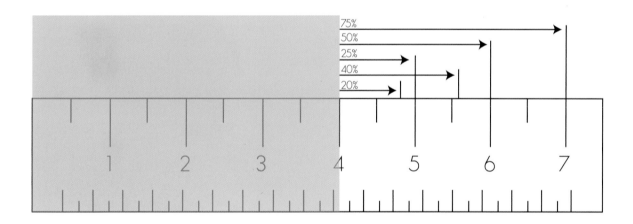

CHOOSING
A NEEDLE

When it comes to sewing projects, the tools you use are of the utmost importance. If you don't use the correct tools, your project could turn into a disaster. I've seen far too many people give up sewing because it was "too hard and complicated." Actually, it's not! Or at least it doesn't have to be. Just like any other hobby, you'll need to have a little bit of know-how before you begin—or your time spent working on said hobby may end up feeling like a waste of time.

In sewing, choosing the correct needle for the project you're working on is extremely important! If you've just taken your brand-new machine out of the box, most likely it's come to you with a universal needle already installed. This needle is great to begin with, but there are other needles that should be used when you begin using different materials for your projects. Here's a breakdown of common needles you may need while sewing your weekend wardrobe:

UNIVERSAL NEEDLE

A general-purpose needle that is great for projects using nonstretch woven fabrics. Great for not-too-thick bag projects, garments using woven fabric, and most everyday sewing.

BALLPOINT NEEDLE

Used with medium-stretch knits. The ballpoint is designed to slide between the fabric fibers and not damage or break them.

STRETCH NEEDLE

Used with high-stretch knits and other elastic fabrics. The specially designed ballpoint helps prevent snags and skipped stitches.

JEANS NEEDLE

This needle is specifically designed to sew through thick woven fabrics (or layers of fabrics and interfacing), such as denim and canvas, without the risk of your needle breaking or stitches being skipped.

TOPSTITCH NEEDLE

Used to topstitch multiple-layered seams without skipping stitches. Great to use when making a bag with many layers of interfacing and fabric.

CHOOSING
A STITCH

After you've chosen the needle you'll be working with, you'll want to choose the perfect stitch. Different stitches are used for different projects and fabrics. Here is a sampling of the stitches I use the most and that are found in this book.

STRAIGHT

A simple, no-fuss stitch used for sewing woven fabrics, this will be the most-used stitch on your machine. You can increase the stitch length for topstitching and shorten it when sewing loosely woven fabrics.

ZIGZAG

These back-and-forth Z-shaped stitches are used when sewing stretch fabrics, locking elastic ends together, etc. Play with the stitch length and width for variations of zigzag stitches to use for different things.

OVERLOCK

Commonly used to describe the stitch created by a serger, the overlock does exactly what it sounds like: it locks (stitches) over the edge of your fabric and encases the raw edge with thread so it does not fray. You do not have to have a serger to overlock your seam allowances, though. Most standard machines come with an overlock stitch selection.

Edge of Fabric

KNIT

The "lightning bolt" stitch on your machine that is used to sew knit fabrics. I prefer this stitch over the zigzag stitch when it comes to sewing most knits. The stitch has built-in stretch that allows stretchy fabrics to move while being worn.

TOP

A stitch that is visible from the right side of the garment. I like to increase the stitch length when I topstitch. Be sure to choose thread that coordinates (or purposely contrasts!) with your fabric.

DECORATIVE

Fancy stitches that can be used for detailing along a neckline, collar, or anywhere really! These stitches may come with your sewing machine and are fun to use in unique ways throughout your apparel.

PDF PATTERNS

PDF patterns are the new normal if you're a part of the sewing community. For years, we all had to rely on big-box brands to produce sewing patterns that may or may not be on trend. Several years ago (right around the time I began my sewing journey), there was a shift in the market and new, self-published pattern designers were popping up left and right. And they were doing something differently: they were offering their patterns as a downloadable file! You no longer had to head to the store, sort through drawers full of patterns, hope they had your size, head home to deal with the mess of tissue paper (hoping nothing tore or blew away!), and figure out how to stuff that thing into the envelope again (tell me I'm not the only one?). Now, with three clicks of your mouse, you could have a stack of paper in your hands ready to dive into that project that you just had to start at midnight.

PDF patterns really did revolutionize the modern sewing industry. If you aren't familiar with them, it isn't too late! Here are my tips for working with PDF patterns:

1. Have access to a good printer. Any home printer will work, but a black-and-white laser printer will give you fast and fairly inexpensive results. The toner lasts a long time, and the pages print at lightning speed.

2. Open all pattern pages in Adobe Reader. If you don't have this program, you can download it for free at https://get.adobe.com/reader/. Print your pattern with the following settings: Size: Custom Scale: 100 percent. Start by printing the first page of the pattern. There will be a 1" × 1" (2.5 × 2.5 cm) and a 2" × 2" (5 × 5 cm) box for you to measure. Be sure the boxes measure exactly! (If you're using a tape measure, start at the 1" [2.5 cm] mark and measure to the 2" [5 cm] mark; this will give you a more exact read.)

3. Your pages can be printed on US Letter (8½" × 11") or A4 (21 × 29.7 cm) paper. The bounding box (the rectangle drawn around the edges of each page to be used as a guide when taping your pattern pieces together) for each page is 7" × 10" (18 cm × 25.5 cm), so the pages will print nicely wherever in the world you are printing!

4. Once your pattern pages are printed out, you'll need to assemble them. See Figure 1 on the following page for an example of how a pattern looks after assembly. To assemble your pattern, cut along the black line on the TOP and LEFT sides of each page. Using the gray squares as guides, align the pages so the pattern lines continue. Tape them together as you go, and soon you'll have one giant pattern page. Each pattern includes a layout guide so you can see how the pages of the PDF go together before you begin taping.

5. You can use pattern tracing paper to trace your size OR you can simply cut out the size you want to use. Remember, since these are PDFs you're able to print and reprint as many times as you'd like!

Tip

If your computer doesn't have a disc drive, you can download the patterns here: www.sewdaily.com/WeekendStylePatterns

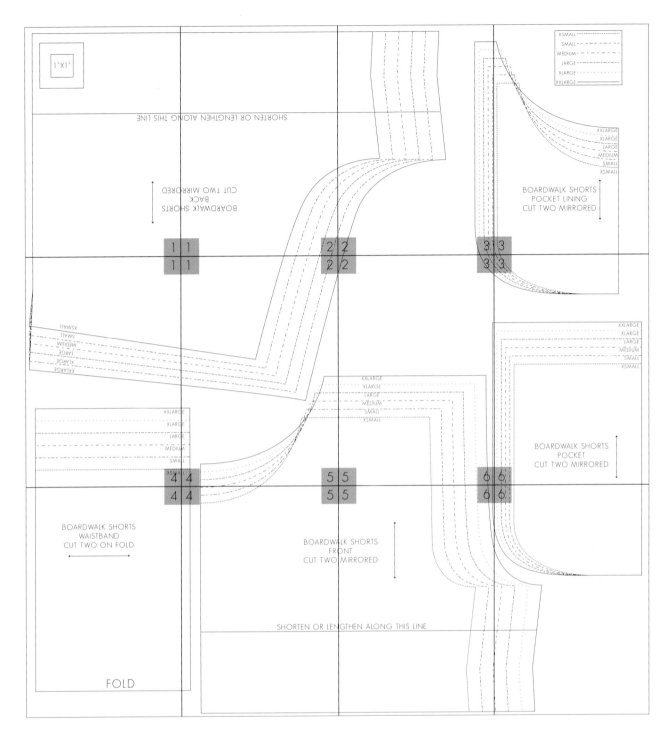

Figure 1

PATTERN SIZING AND ADJUSTMENTS

This book is filled with clothing patterns that are graded from sizes XSmall to XXLarge and sizes 0 to 22 for the two skirt patterns. See below for the size chart we've used for all the garment patterns in this book. Each pattern will advise you on which measurements to use to determine the size you need to sew.

	BUST		WAIST		HIPS	
	Inches	CM	Inches	CM	Inches	CM
XSmall	31	78	24 ½	62	34	86
Small	33 ¾	85	27 ¼	69	36 ¾	93
Medium	36 ½	92	30	76	39 ½	100
Large	39 ¼	100	32 ¾	84	42 ¼	108
XLarge	42	107	35 ½	91	45	115
XXLarge	44 ¾	114	38 ¼	98	47 ¾	122

WAIST MEASUREMENTS FOR SKIRTS					
Size	Inches	CM	Size	Inches	CM
0	24 ½	62	12	32	82
2	25 ¾	65	14	33 ¼	85
4	27	67	16	34 ½	88
6	28 ¼	71	18	35 ¾	91
8	29 ½	75	20	37	95
10	30 ¾	78	22	38 ¼	98

MEASURING YOURSELF

To properly measure yourself, do so undressed with only your undergarments on. Use a soft measuring tape and be sure the tape remains level all the way around your body. You want to pull the tape so it lies flat around your body—not tight, but also with no slack.

The bust is measured around the fullest part of your chest. The waist is measured at your natural waist, typically directly above the navel. The hips are measured at the fullest part of your hips (Figure 1)

ADJUSTING THE PATTERN PIECES

You may be wondering how to determine if a pattern needs adjusting before you begin. The patterns in this book were drafted based on average heights and sizes of women. Most of the garments are loose-fitting, comfortable pieces that won't need any major tailoring. The shorts patterns should be sewn based on your hip measurement and corresponding size, the skirts based on your waist, and the dresses based on your bust and hips. Each pattern includes a shortening or lengthening line.

To adjust the length of the patterns in this book, you'll change the front and back pieces of the pattern only. First, cut along the shorten/lengthen line marked on your pattern pieces (Figure 2). Next, separate the pattern piece and add pattern tracing

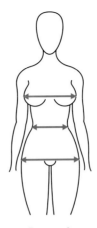

Figure 1

paper or regular paper behind the pattern pieces. Tape the pattern pieces to the paper and connect the lines (Figure 3). Trim off the excess paper along the connecting lines (Figure 4). Cut your pattern out again and be sure to add the SAME length to the opposite pattern piece. To shorten the pattern pieces, overlap the pieces instead of separating.

The patterns in this book are designed with plenty of ease for easy, everyday wear, so if you fall between sizes, I would suggest sizing down. If you fall more than two size differences between measurements, it may be beneficial to you to grade between sizes. For example, if your bust measures a Small and your hips measure a Large and you're sewing one of the dress patterns from this book, you'll want to cut the bust at a Small and ease your cutting out to a Large at the hips.

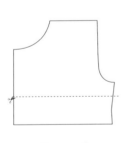

Figure 2

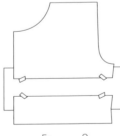

Figure 3

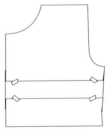

Figure 4

finishing techniques

When a garment is sewn, there are many different ways the raw edges (on the inside and outside) can be finished. Here's a rundown of the techniques we will use in this book. A lot of them are interchangeable and can be used depending on your preference! Finishing your garments leads to a more professional-looking article of clothing, so don't skip out on this part of the project.

NECKLINES AND ARMHOLES

When I first began sewing patterns, the most daunting thing to me was finishing the necklines and armholes. It seems that all pattern designers want you to finish their patterns a different way. I want to share with you my favorite ways to finish necklines and armholes in hopes that you can learn which one works best for you! Once you figure out your favorite and perfect it (read: practice, practice, practice!), you are sure to produce garments that look professionally made. Note: Throughout these instructions I refer to necklines only, but these same techniques can also be used for sleeveless top armholes.

NARROW BIAS FACING
(as used with the Button-Up Tank on page 70)

This is my favorite way to finish necklines and armholes of woven blouses (and you will see this technique used throughout the majority of this book). The clean finish leaves the front of the garment smooth with only a bit of topstitching around the neck and arms. Here's how you do it:

1. Start with a small square piece of fabric (a fat quarter would work great!) and cut on the bias (a 45-degree* angle) strips of fabric that measure 1¼" (3.2 cm) wide. Cut several until they start becoming too short (Figure 1).

Figure 1

2. Sew these strips together by placing them right sides together, creating a 90-degree angle at the short ends on the far-right side of the horizontal strip. Sew from the top-left corner to the bottom-right corner. Snip the seam allowance (Figure 2).

   *Alternatively, you can use pre-made single fold bias tape to create this same result. However, I've found that using this technique gives you a unique finish and takes very little extra time.

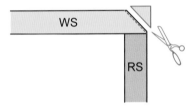

Figure 2

3. Align this long bias strip right sides together with the neckline of your garment. I like starting at the center back for necklines or at the bottom of an armhole. Stitch in place, starting 1" (2.5 cm) from the end of the bias strip (leave that fabric loose) at ⅜" (1 cm) seam allowance (Figure 3).

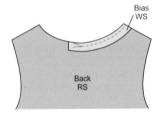

Figure 3

Tip
Use up all of your scraps to make loads of bias to grab when you need it!

4. When you reach about 1" (2.5 cm) away from your starting point, trim your ends so they overlap by ³/₈" (1 cm). Move the ends of the bias strip away from the garment and with right sides facing, sew the short ends together at ³/₈" (1 cm). Finger press that seam allowance open, lay it back along the neckline of the garment, and finish stitching the bias to the neckline (Figure 4). Alternatively, if your garment has an opening, leave a ¹/₂" (1.3 cm) overhang at the beginning and the end. Tuck and press this ¹/₂" (1.3 cm) in toward the garment before proceeding.

5. Trim the seam allowance you just made to about ¹/₄" (6 mm) and clip the curves, being sure not to clip the stitching (Figure 5).

6. Press the seam allowance toward the bias strip (Figure 6).

7. At this point it may be easiest for you to turn your garment inside out and work from the wrong side. Fold the narrow bias strip toward the wrong side and create a clean, sharp edge at the neckline. The seam should be right along the edge of the fold. Press this in place, using pins if necessary (Figure 7).

8. Stitch along the folded edge of the narrow bias strip as close to the fold as you can, smoothing and pulling taut as you go. Note that the thread you use for this step will be seen from the right side of the garment, so be sure it is a color that matches (Figure 8).

9. Turn your garment right side out and press the neckline flat (Figure 9).

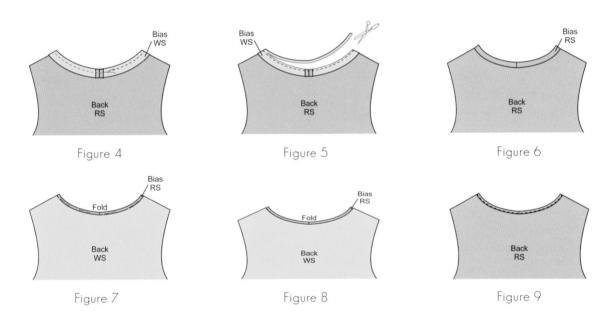

Figure 4

Figure 5

Figure 6

Figure 7

Figure 8

Figure 9

BIAS BINDING

This technique is a great option if you want a contrast fabric to be used along the neckline. This technique can be used when working with knits or wovens. If you are working with knits, however, you won't need to cut your strips on the bias. You'll need to cut them with the stretchiest part of the fabric going lengthwise with the strips.

1. Start with a small square piece of fabric (a fat quarter would work great!) and cut on the bias (a 45-degree angle) strips of fabric that measure 1/2–2" (1.3–5 cm) wide, depending on the bias tape maker you are using. Cut several strips until they start becoming too short (Figure 1).

   Bias tape makers help make creating bias tape a cinch! They come in 6 mm, 12 mm, 18 mm and 25 mm. For garments, I typically use the 18 mm maker, so I'll be using that size in this book.

   To decide how wide to cut your bias strips, take the width of the bias tape maker (18 mm) and double it. That comes to about 1 1/2" (3.8 cm).

2. Sew these strips together by placing them right sides together, creating a 90-degree angle at the short ends on the far-right side of the horizontal strip. Sew from the top-left corner to the bottom-right corner. Snip the seam allowance (Figure 2). Press the seam open.

3. To use your bias tape maker, insert one end of the bias strip with the wrong side facing up through the widest end of the bias tape maker. As it comes out the other end, have your iron ready and press the folds toward the center before they unfold (Figure 3). When the entire piece has gone through the bias tape maker, fold it in half lengthwise so the folded ends meet. Press in place.*

   *Alternatively, you can use pre-made double fold bias tape to create this same result. However, I've found that using the handmade bias tape gives you a unique finish and takes very little extra time.

4. To use this bias tape on the neckline of a garment, unfold the tape and place it right sides together with the neckline of your garment. I like starting at the center back of a neckline or the bottom of an armhole. Start stitching in place starting 1" (2.5 cm) from the end (leave that tape loose) along the fold closest to the neckline or armhole (Figure 4). Alternatively, if your garment has an opening, leave a 1/2" (1.3 cm) overhang at the beginning and the end. Tuck and press this 1/2" (1.3 cm) in toward the garment before proceeding.

Tip

If you are using this technique with a knit, try upcycling an old T-shirt for your knit strips to save on fabric.

5. When you reach about 1" (2.5 cm) away from your starting point, trim your ends so they overlap by $^3/_8$" (1 cm). Move the ends of the bias strip away from the garment and with right sides facing, sew the short ends together at $^3/_8$" (1 cm). Finger press that seam allowance open, lay it back along the neckline or armhole of the garment, and finish stitching the bias to it (Figure 5).

6. Fold the other edge of the bias binding back how it was pressed, bringing the folded edge to the wrong side and aligning it right below the stitch line you just created. Pin it in place if necessary and stitch in the ditch along the edge of the bias tape (Figure 6). I like to do this stitching from the right side of the garment so I am sure that I am stitching in the ditch; this way, the stitch line is hidden in the seam!

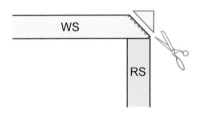

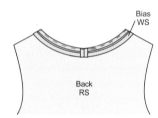

Figure 1

Figure 4

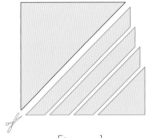

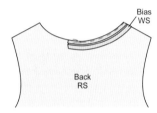

Figure 2

Figure 5

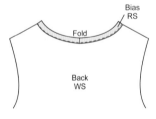

Figure 3

Figure 6

T-SHIRT NECKLINE
(as used with the Tilly Tee on page 42)

This is my favorite way to finish the neckline of a knit garment. It gives a professional, clean finish, and it stretches with the neckline to make it easy for you to take it on and off! You can apply this technique by using your serger or regular sewing machine. If using your regular sewing machine, be sure the stitch you select is the proper stitch for sewing with knits.

1. Cut a straight strip of knit fabric from selvedge to selvedge that is 2" (5 cm) wide, with the stretchiest part of the knit running lengthwise along the strip you've either measured or that you cut from the pattern (Figure 1).

2. Fold the strip in half lengthwise and press (Figure 2). Use spray starch to press your knit in half and hold its shape.

3. Find the two short ends and align them with right sides facing. Stitch them in place at 1/4" (6 mm). Finger press the seam allowance open and fold the neckband back the way it was pressed (Figure 3).

4. Find the "four corners" of the neckband by placing a pin in the center back (the seam), in the center front, and on each side (Figure 4). Do the same for the neckline of the garment. Note: the sides of the neckline are NOT typically at the shoulder seams.

5. Place your neckband on the outside of your garment and align the three raw edges (two from the neckband and one from the garment) at the pins. Pin the neckband in place to the garment (Figure 5). The neckband will be smaller than the neckline..

6. On your serger or sewing machine, stitch the neckband to the neckline by stretching the neckband evenly between each pin (Figure 6). Be careful not to stretch the neckline of the garment while doing so.

7. When finished, press the neckband away from the garment. Using your sewing machine, topstitch the seam allowance to the garment for a nice, professional finish (Figure 7).

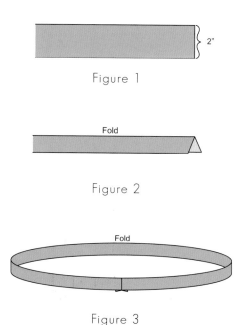

Figure 1

Figure 2

Figure 3

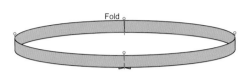

Fold

Figure 4

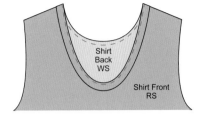

Shirt
Back
WS

Shirt Front
RS

Figure 6

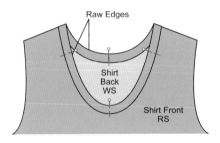

Raw Edges

Shirt
Back
WS

Shirt Front
RS

Figure 5

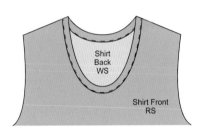

Shirt
Back
WS

Shirt Front
RS

Figure 7

TIP

Some patterns will give you the correct length and width of fabric needed to sew a T-shirt neckband, and some patterns, like the Tilly Tee, include the neckband as a pattern piece. However, if you want to add this technique to a garment that doesn't use it, here are the general instructions: Measure the length of the neckline you're working with, and then multiply that measurement by 85 percent. This will give you the length measurement needed for this neckband. The length varies a bit depending on how stretchy your fabric is, but this is a good rule of thumb. You want to be stretching your neckband as you go.

INSIDE SEAM-ALLOWANCE FINISHES

There are several ways to finish seam allowances on the inside of your garment. It is important to finish these seam allowances so the fabric does not unravel, causing strings to fly everywhere. This extra step is definitely important for garments you plan on wearing a lot.

SERGER

The serger method is the method I most commonly use. A serger machine is in addition to your sewing machine and creates nice, overlocked edges. It has a knife on it, so the seam allowance is trimmed down evenly as the fabric is sent through the machine and the edges are being overlocked. It uses anywhere from two to five cones of thread (depending on the make and model of your machine) and creates a truly professional-looking garment on the inside. Sergers are also great for sewing with knits because of the built-in elasticity in the stitches.

OVERLOCK/ZIGZAG STITCH

If you don't own a serger, this method works great too. While it isn't quite as quick or clean as the serger method, using the zigzag or overlock stitches on your sewing machine will work just as well.

FRENCH SEAMS

If you don't want to see any raw edges or threads on the inside of your garment, then French seams are for you. They take a bit of extra work and stitching, but they are relatively easy to achieve AND have built-in reinforcement to the stitches. One thing to note about French seams is that you'll want to make sure the seam allowance included in the pattern pieces is big enough. A $^5/_8$" (1.5 cm) seam allowance is ideal, but $^1/_2$" (1.3 cm) seams can work as well. For these instructions, I'll be using a $^5/_8$" (1.5 cm) seam allowance. If using a $^1/_2$" (1.3 cm) seam allowance, you will need to decrease your seam allowance in each step by $^1/_8$" (3 mm).

1. Begin by sewing the seam you are working on with the wrong sides together at $^3/_8$" (1 cm) (Figure 1).

2. Trim this seam allowance down to a generous $^1/_8$" (3 mm) (Figure 2) and press to one side.

3. Turn the garment to the inside and press the seams as flat as possible. Sew along this edge at $^1/_4$" (6 mm) (Figure 3).

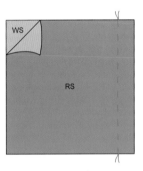

Figure 1

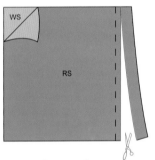

Figure 2

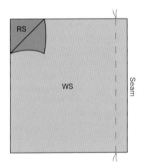

Figure 3

weekend style

From shorts perfect for lounging on a Saturday monring, to a sparkly Date Night skirt, the projects in this chapter have all of your weekend wardrobe needs covered. The detailed, step-by-step instructions will help you through each part of sewing these projects, so you'll have the perfect outfit for whatever the weekend brings in no time!

Tilly Tee

The Tilly Tee is the perfect go-to T-shirt for casual wear. Sew it out of a lightweight knit for a flowy, easy-to-wear tee that will go with practically anything in your wardrobe! The Tilly Tee features loose sleeves, a neckband and a flattering fit through the waist and hips. Try pairing it with the Afternoon Skirt (page 54); this tee will complete any outfit! Choose your size for the Tilly Tee based on your bust measurement.

FABRIC

Type
Lightweight to medium-weight knit such as jersey, rayon, polyester, or other lightweight blends with at least 40 percent stretch

Quantity
54" (137 cm) wide: 1 yard (0.9 m)

OTHER MATERIALS
Tilly Tee pattern: 4 pieces

pattern

1. Align the front and back bodices along the shoulders with right sides facing. Pin and stitch the shoulder seams. Lay the bodice flat with the right side facing up and the bodice pieces not touching.

2. With right sides together, align the center notch on the sleeve with the shoulder seam of the bodice pieces and the other two notches with their matching partners. The double notch goes at the back and the single notch goes at the front.

3. Stitch the sleeve to the armhole opening. Repeat Steps 2 and 3 for the other sleeve.

4. Turn the top to the wrong side and align the sides together. Starting at the hem of the sleeve, pin, and stitch the sleeve and sides (Figure 1).

5. Follow the instructions on page 36 for how to sew a T-shirt neckline.

6. Hem the sleeves by pressing the raw edge toward the wrong side at $^3/_8$" (1 cm) and stitching them in place using a zigzag stitch. Hem the bottom by pressing the raw edge toward the wrong side at $^1/_4$" (6 mm) and again at 1" (2.5 cm). Topstitch it in place using a zigzag stitch (Figure 2).

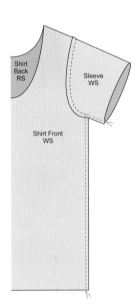

Figure 1

Figure 2

colonial cover-up

The Colonial Cover-Up is an easy-to-sew, casual dress that is perfect for throwing over your swimsuit to head to the beach or pool. Make one in all your favorite prints and wear it all summer long. You can even wear it sans swimsuit as a simple knit sundress. It pairs well with the Turban Twist Headband (page TK) and the Pool Tote (page TK). The Colonial Cover-Up features a simple silhouette made from knit fabric and incorporates a knit binding for finishing raw edges and creating the straps. Choose your size for the Colonial Cover-Up based on your bust and hip measurements.

FABRIC

Type
Lightweight to medium-weight knit such as jersey, rayon, polyester, or other lightweight blends. Your fabric should be drapey/bouncy/flowy, with a good amount of stretch.

Quantity
54" (137 cm) wide:
2¼ yards (2.1 m)
(Less fabric can be used for nondirectional prints.)

OTHER MATERIALS
Knit fabric for binding, ⅛ yard (11.4 cm)

Colonial Cover-Up pattern: 2 pieces

pattern

1. Lay the two main pieces wrong sides together with the sides aligning. Follow the instructions on page 39 to create French seams along the sides.

2. Fold the points where the neckline and armholes meet toward the wrong side at ¼" (6 mm) and stitch in place (Figure 1).

   Make the bias binding out of knit fabric using the instructions on page 34.

3. Find the center of the back bias binding tape and pin it in place at the back center of the cover-up. Using the instructions on page 34, sew the binding to the back neckline of the cover-up. Extend the stitching beyond the neckline by edgestitching the remaining length of the straps (Figure 1).

4. Find the center of the front bias binding tape and pin it in place at the front center of the cover-up. Using the sewing instructions on page 34, sew the binding to the front neckline and armholes of the cover-up. Extend the stitching beyond the armholes by edgestitching the remaining length of the straps)..

5. Try on the dress to determine your desired strap length. Pull the straps to the front: the outer straps will come straight to the front and attach at the outer notches. The inner straps will crisscross and attach at the inner notches (Figure 2).

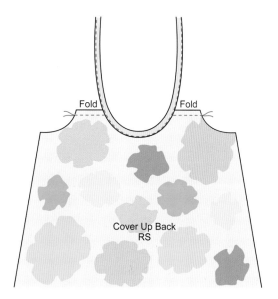

Figure 1

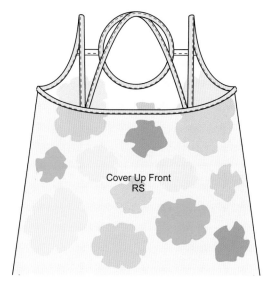

Figure 2

6. Hem the cover-up by pressing the bottom of the dress toward the wrong side at ½" (1.3 cm) and again at ½" (1.3 cm). Stitch close to the upper folded edge (Figure 3).

Figure 3

Larchmont Tee

The Larchmont Tee is an easy-to-sew shirt pattern that features dolman sleeves and a locket closure along the back neckline. When sewn out of the right fabric, this tee can be made and worn a million different ways. It's the perfect "blousy" tee that is just the right amount of fancy and casual to wear shopping with friends. Pair it with your favorite skinny jeans and you're good to go! Choose your size for the Larchmont Tee based on your bust measurement.

FABRIC

Type
Lightweight woven fabric such as chambray, rayon, or voile (anything drapey and swingy)

Quantity
44" (112 cm) wide:
XS-M, 2¼ yards (2.1 m);
L-XXL, 2¼ yards (2.1 m)
54" (137 cm) wide:
XS-M, 1½ yards (1.4 m);
L-XXL, 2¼ yards (2.1 m)

OTHER MATERIALS
Small piece of ⅛" (3 mm) elastic

One ½" (1.3 cm) button

Larchmont Tee pattern: 3 pieces

pattern

1. Lay your top front and back pieces right sides together, aligning the shoulders and side seams. Stitch in place along the shoulders and side seams. Finish these edges with a zig-zag or overlock stitch.

2. Fold and press the sleeve hem at $\frac{1}{4}$" (6 mm) and again at $\frac{1}{4}$" (6 mm). Edgestitch in place along the fold (Figure 1).

3. Turn the shirt right sides out. Fold the $\frac{1}{8}$" (3 mm) elastic in half lengthwise and place it about 1" (2.5 cm) down from the neckline with the raw edges on the stitch line you transferred. Lay the placket piece on the center back of your top, right sides together, aligning the stitch lines. Pin it in place, and sew around the designated stitch line. Be sure to catch the elastic between the top and the placket (Figure 2).

4. Snip in between the stitches on the placket from the neckline to almost the bottom row of stitches, and then at an angle in the corners. Be sure not to snip through the stitches (Figure 3).

5. Fold the placket to the wrong side of the top, and fold the raw edges under so they aren't showing. Press and topstitch in place through all the layers (Figure 4).

6. On the right side of the back of your top, add the button so it can easily be hooked by the elastic.

7. Follow the steps on page 31 for the narrow bias facing to finish the neckline.

8. Fold and press the bottom hem of the top toward the wrong side at $\frac{1}{4}$" (6 mm) and again at $\frac{3}{4}$" (1 cm). Edgestitch in place (Figure 5).

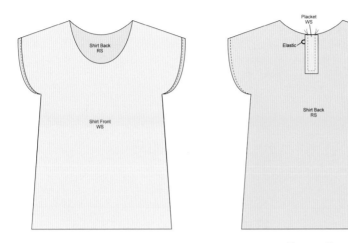

Figure 1

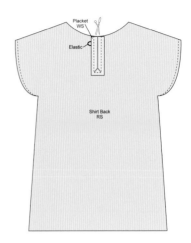

Figure 2

Figure 3

Figure 4

Figure 5

afternoon skirt

The Afternoon Skirt offers so much perfection to a picnic-in-the-park kind of day. This skirt can easily be sewn in an array of different fabrics and features a button-down front closure. The skirt also has two optional, deep front pockets for functional or aesthetic use. Pair it with a Tilly Tee (page 42) and your favorite pair of sandals or Converse sneakers and enjoy your afternoon. Choose your size for the Afternoon Skirt based on your waist measurement.

FABRIC

Type
Lightweight to medium-weight woven fabric such as quilting cotton, chambray, lightweight denim, rayon, or voile

Quantity
44" (112 cm) wide:
All sizes, 2 yards (1.8 m)
54" (137 cm) wide:
XS-M, 1⅝ yards (1.5 m);
L-XXL, 1⅞ yards (1.7 m)

OTHER MATERIALS
Fusible interfacing (such as Pellon SF101), 20" (51 cm) wide, ⅓ yard (0.3 m)

Buttonhole foot

Six ½" (1.3 cm) buttons

Afternoon Skirt pattern: 5 pieces

pattern

1. Lay your skirt back piece right-side up and align the skirt front pieces so the skirt back and skirt fronts are right sides together and the outer edges align. Pin the side seams in place. Stitch along the pinned edges. Finish your seams using a zigzag stitch or serger.

2. Stitch two rows of basting stitches at $\frac{1}{8}$" (3 mm) and $\frac{1}{4}$" (6 mm) along the top edge of the skirt. Gather the skirt using the waistband as a guide on how wide the top of the skirt should be. Wrap the gathering thread around the pins to temporarily hold the gathering. Align the two marks/notches on the waistband with the side seams of the skirt (Figure 1).

3. Align the waistband front to the top of the skirt with right sides facing. Adjust the gathering evenly around the skirt as needed. Pin it in place and stitch (Figure 2). Press the waistband and seam allowance up.

4. Press the bottom edge of the waistband lining toward the wrong side at $\frac{1}{4}$" (6 mm). Pin it with the unfolded edge aligned with the top edge of the waistband front, right sides together (Figure 3). Stitch along the pinned edge and press this seam allowance toward the waistband.

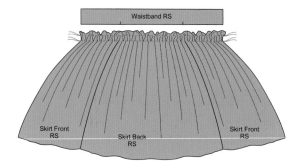

Figure 1

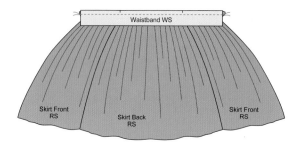

Figure 2

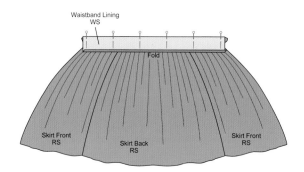

Figure 3

5. Flip the waistband lining toward the inside of the skirt and press the top seam for a nice, flat finish. The folded edge of the waistband lining should fall just below the waistband stitch line. Pin the waistband in place and flip your skirt to the right side. Stitch in the ditch of the waistband, being sure to catch the waistband lining on the wrong side. Remove pins as you go.

6. Press all edges of the pocket (except for the top) toward the wrong side at ¼" (6 mm). Fold the top edge of a pocket piece down ¼" (6 mm) and again ¼" (6 mm). Press and topstitch in place (Figure 4). Repeat for the second pocket.

7. Lay the pockets on the skirt on top of the designated markers. Pin them and edgestitch in place along the sides and bottom.

   Hem your skirt by folding and pressing the bottom hem toward the wrong side at 1" (2.5 cm) and again at 1" (2.5 cm). Topstitch in place. Be sure to catch the edge of the hem on the wrong side of the skirt.

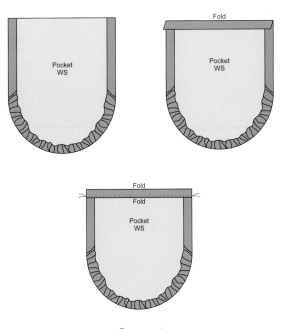

Figure 4

10. Flip the placket toward the inside of the skirt along the placket's centerline and press the edge seam for a nice, flat finish. The inner folded edge of the placket should fall just to the right of the placket stitch line (Figure 6). Pin the placket in place and flip your skirt to the right side. Stitch in the ditch of the placket, being sure to catch the placket lining on the wrong side. Remove pins as you go (Figure 7).

    Repeat Steps 8-10 for the left side of the skirt. You will use the non-interfaced placket piece.

11. Press the placket and transfer the buttonhole markings from the buttonhole marker template to the right placket (left as you are facing). Using the buttonhole foot on your sewing machine, sew the buttonholes. Use a seam ripper to very carefully make slits in the buttonholes (Figure 8).

    Mark on the left side (right as you are facing) the button placement and attach the buttons by using your button attachment foot on your sewing machine or by hand-sewing them to your skirt.

12. Button up your skirt and admire your work (Figure 9)!

8. Add interfacing to one of the plackets per the manufacturer's instructions. Align the interfaced placket piece with the right side (left side as you are facing) of the skirt with right sides facing. Pin and stitch it in place at $^3/_8$" (1 cm). Press this seam allowance toward the placket (Figure 5).

9. Fold and press the opposite edge of the placket at $^3/_8$" (1 cm) toward the wrong side.

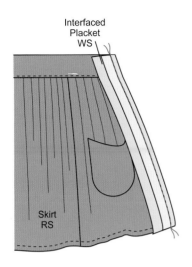

Interfaced
Placket
WS

Skirt
RS

Figure 5

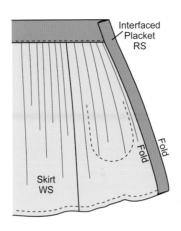

Interfaced
Placket
RS

Skirt
WS

Fold

Figure 6

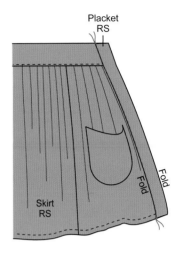

Placket
RS

Skirt
RS

Fold

Fold

Figure 7

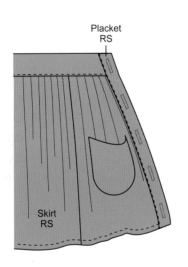

Placket
RS

Skirt
RS

Figure 8

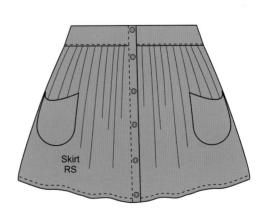

Skirt
RS

Figure 9

boardwalk shorts

Sew the Boardwalk Shorts in an afternoon, slip them on, and head out anywhere and everywhere. Easy to style with a simple tee (try the Tilly Tee on page 42) or a tank, these shorts will be your go-to all spring and summer. The Boardwalk Shorts feature an elastic waistband to create a paper-bag-style gathered waist. Sew up a Tie-On Belt to complete the look. Choose your size for the Boardwalk Shorts based on your hip measurement.

FABRIC

Type
Medium-weight to heavyweight fabric such as denim, chambray, canvas, or cotton

Quantity
44" (112 cm) wide:
All Sizes, 1 1/2 yards (1.4 m)
54" (137 cm) wide:
All Sizes, 1 1/8 yards (1 m)

OTHER MATERIALS

1 package 3/4" (2 cm) knit elastic

Large safety pin

Boardwalk Shorts pattern: 5 pieces

pattern

1. Finish the outer curve of your pocket and pocket-lining pieces with zigzag stitching, with serge/overlock stitching, or by using pinking shears.

2. Lay one of your shorts front pieces right-side up and place the matching pocket-lining piece right-side down aligning the concave edge. Pin and stitch the lining in place at $^3/_8$" (1 cm) (Figure 1). Clip the curve, turn the lining to the wrong side of the shorts front, and press the lining in place so you have a nice seam.

3. Topstitch this seam at $^1/_4$" (6 mm) from the edge.

4. Choose one of two methods to attach your pockets:

    A. Lay your shorts front piece right-side down and lay the matching pocket piece right-side down on top of it, aligning the top and side edges with the top and side edges of the shorts. Pin and baste the edges in place. Sew along the convex (outer) edge of the pocket and pocket-lining pieces about $^1/_4$" (6 mm) from the edge so they are sewn to the front of the shorts (Figure 2).

    B. Another option for the pockets on your shorts is to pull the pocket and pocket-lining piece away from the shorts and pin them together. Instead of sewing the pocket and pocket lining to the shorts front, sew only the pocket to the pocket lining and then baste along the side and top.

    Repeat Steps 2–4 for the other side of the shorts.

5. Align one shorts front and one shorts back piece right sides together with the inseam edges matching. Pin and stitch in place. Finish this seam and press toward the back

6. Align the side edges of the same shorts front and back pieces, pin, and stitch in place. Finish this seam and press to the back (Figure 3).

    Repeat Steps 5 and 6 for the second set of shorts front and back pieces.

7. Turn one set of shorts front and back pieces to the right side. Insert this set inside the other so the right sides are facing and both sets of seams align. Pin and sew along the "U" shape that has been created (Figure 4). Finish this seam with a serger, or clip the curves and press the seam open. Turn the shorts to the right side.

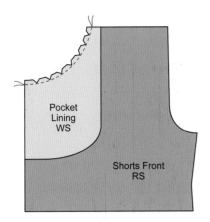

Figure 1

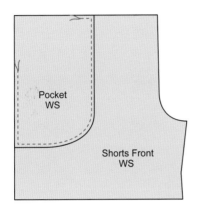

Figure 2

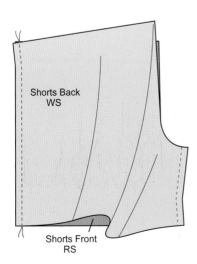

Figure 3

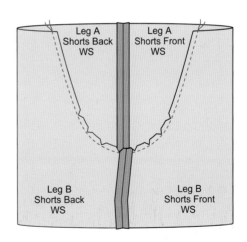

Figure 4

8. Align the two waistband pieces right sides together, and sew along the short ends. This will create a large loop. Fold the raw edges together so that the wrong sides are facing. Press in place (Figure 5).

9. Stitch 1" (2.5 cm) from the top all the way around the folded waistband piece. Stitch 1" (2.5 cm) below this stitch line all the way around the folded waistband piece leaving about a 2" (5 cm) opening to insert elastic (Figure 6).

10. Align the two raw edges of your waistband piece to the top raw edges of your shorts, matching the side seams. Pin and sew the waistband in place leaving about a 2" (5 cm) opening to insert elastic (Figure 7).

11. Attach the safety pin to your 3/4" (2 cm) knit elastic and insert it into the casing. Use this to shimmy the elastic all the way around through the casing. When the elastic is fully inserted, overlap the two ends by 1/2" (1.3 cm) and stitch them together. Finish sewing the waistband to the shorts where you left the 2" (5 cm) opening and finish the bottom stitch line on the waistband as well, being careful not to sew the elastic to the shorts.

12. To hem the shorts, press the bottom raw edge to the wrong side at 1/4" (6 mm) and then again at 1" (2.5 cm) and topstitch in place (Figure 8).

Figure 5

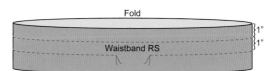

Figure 6

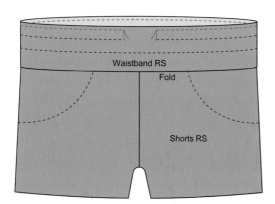

Figure 7

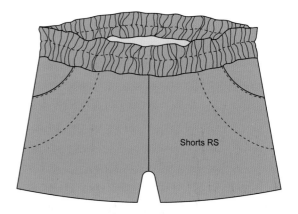

Figure 8

date night skirt

Everyone needs a go-to outfit for date night with their significant other, and what could be better than a sewing pattern that can give you a fancy OR casual look? Choose a dressy or casual fabric, depending on your style, and pair it with the Larchmont Tee (page 50) and wedges for the perfect evening out. The Date Night Skirt features a fitted waistband at your natural waist, constructed with a zipper for easy wear. Choose your size for the Date Night Skirt based on your waist measurement.

FABRIC

Type
Lightweight to medium-weight woven fabric such as quilting cotton, chambray, rayon, voile, or lightweight denim

Quantity
44" (112 cm) wide:
XS–M: 1³/₄ yards (1.6 m);
L–XXL: 2 yards (1.8 m)
54" (137 cm) wide:
XS–M: 1³/₄ yards (1.6 m);
L–XXL: 2 yards (1.8 m)

OTHER MATERIALS

One 12"–14" (30.5 cm–35.6 cm) zipper that coordinates with your fabric

Fusible interfacing (such as Pellon SF101), 20" (51 cm) wide, ¹/₃ yard (0.3 m)

Date Night Skirt pattern: 2 pieces

pattern

1. Add interfacing to the waistband per the manufacturer's instructions. Align the waistband front to the top of the skirt with right sides facing. Pin it in place and stitch (Figure 1). Press this seam allowance toward the waistband.

2. Press the bottom edge of the waistband lining toward the wrong side at $\frac{1}{4}$" (6 mm). Pin it with the unfolded edge aligned with the top edge of the waistband front, right sides together. Stitch along the pinned edge (Figure 2) and press this seam allowance toward the waistband.

3. Lay your skirt right side facing up with the waistband and waistband lining flat. Finish the back edges of the skirt with an overlock or zigzag stitch.

4. Place a zipper right-side down aligning the top of the teeth with the stitch line between the waistband and waistband lining. Align the edge with the raw edge of the skirt, adjusting the zipper so when sewn it will maintain a $\frac{1}{2}$" (1.3 cm) seam allowance. Pin the zipper in place and stitch it as far as the bottom of the teeth. (Figure 3). Repeat this for the other side of the zipper.

5. With right sides of the skirt together, sew the remainder of the back seam below the zipper. Be sure to start exactly where you stopped when inserting the zipper so there is no gap (Figure 4).

6. Press the seam allowance open.

7. Flip the waistband lining toward the inside of the skirt and press the top seam for a nice, flat finish. The folded edge of the waistband lining should fall just below the waistband stitch line. Pin the waistband in place and flip your skirt to the right side. Stitch in the ditch of the waistband, being sure to catch the waistband on the wrong side. Remove pins as you go (Figure 5).

Figure 1

Figure 2

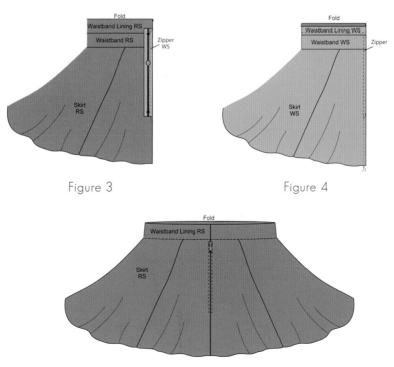

Figure 3

Figure 4

Figure 5

button-up tank

The Button-Up Tank is a casual top that can easily transition from day to night. It features a loose-fitting style that buttons up the front for easy wear and construction. Tuck it into a pair of Boardwalk Shorts (page 60) or let it hang loose over a pair of jeans. The Button-Up Tank will easily become a staple in your wardrobe. Try pairing it with the Date Night Skirt (page 66) or Afternoon Skirt (page 54) for a perfectly handmade outfit. Choose your size for the Button-Up Tank based on your bust measurement.

FABRIC

Type

Lightweight to medium-weight woven fabric such as quilting cotton, chambray, lightweight denim, rayon, or voile

Quantity

44" (112 cm) wide;
All sizes, 1³/₄ yards (1.6 m)

54" (137 cm) wide;
All sizes, 1³/₄ yards (1.6 m)

OTHER MATERIALS

Fusible interfacing (such as Pellon), 20" (51 cm) wide, ¹/₃ yard (0.3 m)

Six ¹/₂" (1.3 cm) buttons

Button-Up Tank pattern: 5 pieces

pattern

1. Lay the back piece right-side up. Fold and press the pleat lines toward the center back of the top. Baste this pleat in place (Figures 1 and 2).

2. Sandwich the back piece between the two yoke pieces in this order: yoke right-side up, back right side up, yoke wrong-side up (Figure 3).

3. Align along the straight edges, pin, and sew in place (Figure 4).

4. Press the yoke pieces away from the back piece and topstitch $1/4$" (6 mm) above the stitch line on the yoke. Set this piece aside (Figure 5).

5. Take the button placket and align the strip of interfacing between the dashed lines. Fuse it in place on the WRONG side of the fabric.

    Lay the front pieces right-side up. On the left (facing the top pieces), place the interfaced button placket right sides together matching the edges. Stitch in place at $3/8$" (1 cm) (Figure 6).

6. Turn the top to the wrong side and press the seam allowance toward the button placket. At this time, press the placket's other raw edge under at $3/8$" (1 cm) (Figure 7).

7. Pull the pressed edge just barely over the seam and press it in place. Flip the front piece to the right side and stitch in the ditch of the seam allowance you created. This should sew the placket in place.

    Repeat Steps 5-7 for the other front piece, except do not use interfacing on this side (Figure 8).

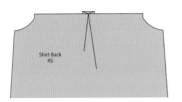

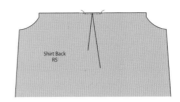

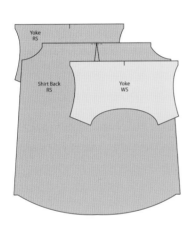

Figure 1

Figure 2

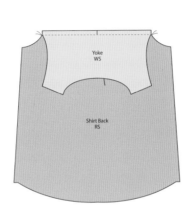

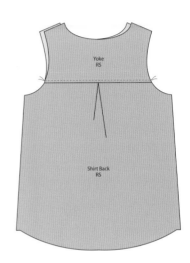

Figure 3

Figure 4

Figure 5

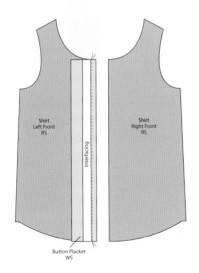

Figure 6

Figure 7

Figure 8

8. Lay the back piece right side up and lay the two front pieces right sides down, aligning the outside yoke piece at the shoulders. Allow the other yoke piece to hang loose. Pin and baste in place at ¹/₄" (6 mm) (Figure 9).

9. Burrito-roll the front and back bodice pieces of the top. Flip the inside yoke piece that is hanging loose so its right side is facing the right side of the front yolk and align at the shoulders (the top will be rolled up, sandwiched inside the yoke pieces). Stitch in place along the shoulders below the basting stitch you created in Step 8 (Figure 10).

10. Pull the bodices out through the neck and press the shoulder seam allowance. Topstitch in place along the back yoke shoulder seam at ¹/₄" (6 mm) from the seam (Figure 11).

11. Align the front and back bodices along the sides, right sides together. Pin and stitch in place.

12. Follow the steps listed on page 31 for a narrow bias facing around the neckline and the armholes. On the ends of the neckline, be sure to fold the edges of the ends in so there are no raw edges showing.

13. Using the buttonhole stitch on your machine, add the buttonholes on the left (facing the top pieces).

14. Add the buttons to the right (facing the top).

    Hem the top by pressing along the bottom edge at ¹/₄" (6 mm) toward the wrong side and again at ¹/₂" (1.3 cm). Topstitch in place (Figure 12).

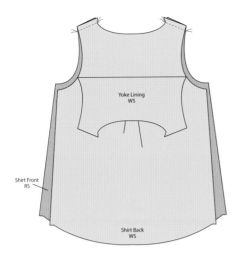

Figure 9

Figure 10

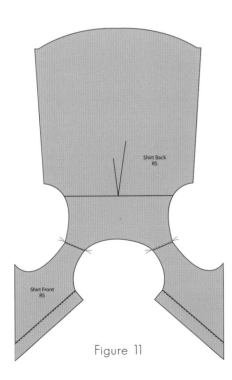

Figure 11

Figure 12

saturday morning shorts

Saturday mornings are for lounging around, drinking coffee, reading a book, and drinking more coffee. This sewing pattern makes the perfect pair of lounging shorts for you to wear and love. The Saturday Morning Shorts feature an elastic and drawstring waistband and the option to add a fun pom-pom trim to the hem. Pair these shorts with the Tilly Tee (page 42) to complete your look. Choose your size for the Saturday Morning Shorts based on your hip measurement.

FABRIC

Type

Lightweight to medium-weight woven fabric such as quilting cotton, voile, or double gauze

Quantity

44" (112 cm) wide:
All sizes, 1 yard (0.9 m)
54" (137 cm) wide:
All sizes, 1 yard (0.9 m)

OTHER MATERIALS

Pom-pom trim, 2 yards (1.8 m) (optional)

½" (1.3 cm) twill tape, 2-3 yards (1.8-2.7 m) (optional, in lieu of a fabric drawstring)

1 package ¾" (2 cm) knit elastic

Safety pin

Saturday Morning Shorts pattern: 2 pieces

pattern

1. Align one shorts front and one shorts back piece right sides together with the inseam edges matching. Pin and stitch the inseam in place. Clip the curves and press the seam open.

2. Align the outer edges of that same shorts front and back piece right sides together. Pin and stitch the side seams in place (Figure 1). Press the seams open. Repeat Steps 1 and 2 for the second set of shorts front and back pieces.

3. Turn one set of shorts front and back pieces to the right side. Insert this set inside the other so the right sides are facing and both sets of seams align. Pin and sew along the "U" shape that has been created. Clip the curves and press the seam open (Figure 2).

   Turn the shorts to the right side and stitch the buttonholes where the markings were transferred.

4. Turn the shorts wrong-side out. Fold and press the very top edge of the shorts (what will become the waist-band) to the wrong side at $1/4$" (6 mm)*, and then again at $1 1/4$" (3.2 cm). Topstitch $1/8$" (3 mm) away from the top folded edge and $1/8$" (3 mm) away from the bottom edge. Along the bottom edge, leave about a 2" (5 cm) opening for adding elastic (Figure 3).

Attach a large safety pin to one end of the knit elastic, insert it into the casing, and shimmy it through. When the elastic is fully inserted, overlap the two ends by $1/2$" (1.3 cm) and stitch them together. Sew the opening on the shorts closed so the elastic stays inside the casing.

   *Optional: Add additional lines of stitching $1/4$" (6 mm) away (below the top and above the bottom) from each of the first stitch lines to hold the elastic in place. Do so by stretching the elastic as you sew around the waistband of the shorts, being careful to stretch the elastic uniformly all the way around.

5. Hem the shorts by turning the bottom toward the wrong side at $1/4$" (6 mm) and again at $1/4$" (6 mm). Stitch the hem in place.

   Optional: Add the pom-pom trim by topstitching both edges of the twill to the right side of the shorts right along the stitch line of the hem.

6. To make the drawstring from fabric, take your 2" (5 cm) strip of fabric and fold and press the strip wrong sides together down the length. Unfold and then fold the long edges toward the center and press. Then fold the pressed edges to one another. Top-stitch along the long edge where the folded edges meet (Figure 4).

7. Attach the safety pin to the draw-string and insert it through the buttonholes. Trim to your liking, leaving enough length to tie a bow. Tie off the ends with a knot (Figure 5).

Tie your shorts in a bow and enjoy your Saturday morning!

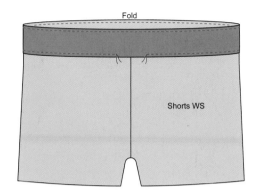

Figure 3

Figure 1

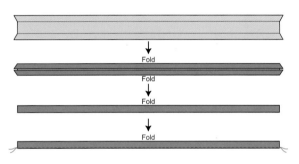

Figure 4

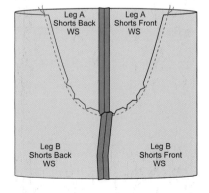

Figure 2

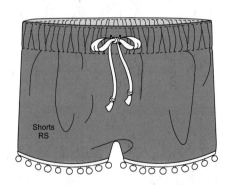

Figure 5

darling shift dress

There is nothing quite as perfect as putting on a simple dress to easily scoot from brunch with friends to errands around town to a date night with your man. Slip on the Darling Shift Dress and conquer your day in style! This comfortable dress features a zipper in the back, half-length sleeves, and a gathered bottom tier for flounce. Choose your size for the Darling Shift Dress based on your bust and hip measurements.

FABRIC

Type

Lightweight woven fabric such as chambray, rayon, or voile (anything drapey and swingy)

Quantity

44" (112 cm) wide:
All sizes, 3 yards (2.7 m)
54" (137 cm) wide:
All sizes, 2³/₈ yards (2.2 m)

OTHER MATERIALS

Fusible interfacing (such as Pellon), 20" (51 cm) wide, ¹/₃ yard (0.3 m)

One 14" (35.5 cm) zipper that coordinates with your fabric

Darling Shift Dress pattern:
6 pieces

pattern

1. Sew the darts on the front pieces of the dress. You'll do this by aligning the dart markings to one another and sewing a straight line on the wrong side of the fabric. Taper your stitch off at the end and do not backstitch. Instead, leave a tail of thread and tie a knot to secure the stitches in place. When both darts have been sewn, press the dart seam allowance toward the hem of the dress (Figure 1).

2. Lay the front of the dress right-side up, and align the two back pieces on top of the front piece, aligning at the shoulders with right sides facing down. Pin and stitch the shoulder seams in place. Finish these seams (see page 39) and press the seam allowances toward the back.

3. Prepare your sleeve pieces by sewing two rows of basting stitches at $1/8$" (3 mm) and $1/4$ (6 mm) from the raw edge along the curve between the two notches. Gather between these notches. Twist the threads around pins to hold the gathers in place. Lay the dress flat, right-sides up. Align the sleeve along the opening, right-side down, matching the three notches. Distribute the gathers evenly. Pin and stitch in place. Finish this seam and press toward the dress (Figure 2).

4. Place the sleeve and dress right sides together, making sure the sleeve seams align. Pin and stitch in place from the sleeve hem to the bottom of the dress. Finish this seam and press to one side.

   Repeat Steps 3 and 4 for the other sleeve. Finish the center back edges of the two back panels of your dress.

5. To prepare to add the zipper, lay the dress flat with your zipper on top of it. The top metal stopper should be right at the raw edge of the dress neckline. Mark on your dress the spot where the bottom metal stopper of the zipper sits. Align the two back panels of your dress right sides together. From the bottom, sew up to the mark you made on your dress and backstitch. From this point to the top of your neckline, sew using a BASTING stitch (so it will be easy to remove later!). Press this seam open (Figure 3).

6. Place your zipper right side down on the wrong side of the dress, being careful to align it perfectly with your basting stitches. Set your machine back to a regular length stitch and attach a zipper foot. Stitch the zipper to the seam allowance (be careful not to sew through the front of your dress!). Stitch all the way around the zipper teeth. Flip your dress over and carefully remove the basting stitches (Figure 4).

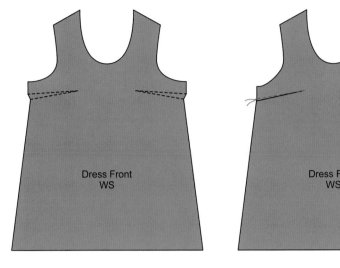

Figure 1

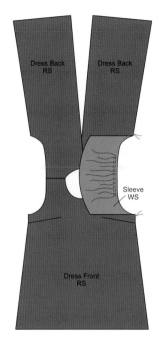

Figure 2

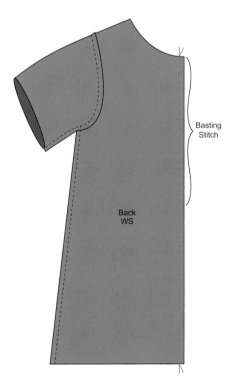

Basting
Stitch

Figure 3

Figure 4

7. Stitch the interfacing to the facing. Finish the outer edge of your facing piece. Place it right sides together around the neckline of your dress, being sure to align it to the center of your neckline (there will be overhang on the ends) (Figure 5).

8. Stitch the facing to the neckline. Fold the overhang on the ends toward the wrong side so the raw edges will be enclosed when you flip the facing over. Clip the curves. Press the seam allowance toward the facing and stitch at $1/4$" (6 mm) to the facing (this will help the facing to stay flat). Flip the facing to the wrong side and press the seams so they have a nice finish. Optional (but preferred by me): Stitch the inner edge of the facing to the neckline of the dress.

9. Align the skirt portions of your dress right sides together. Stitch along the short ends to create one large loop. Press the seams open.

   Fold the loop so the wrong sides are facing, aligning the raw edge. Stitch two rows of basting stitches along the top of the raw edge, one at $1/4$" (6 mm) and one at $1/8$" (3 mm). Pull the threads and gather the skirt portion of your dress until the width matches the width of the bottom of your dress. Twist the threads around pins to hold the gathers in place.

   Align the gathered edge to the bottom of the dress. Match the side seams, distributing the gathers evenly. Pin and sew the ruffle in place (Figure 6).

10. To add the sleeve cuffs, first fold a cuff piece right sides together matching the short ends, and stitch in place to create a loop. Press this seam open. Along one edge of the cuff, press the edge $1/4$" (6 mm) to the wrong side. Align the other edge of the cuff, right sides facing, to the sleeve opening. Pin and stitch in place. Press this seam allowance toward the cuff (Figure 7).

11. Fold the cuff to the wrong side of the sleeve and align the folded/pressed edge of the cuff right above the stitch line. Press the fold and stitch in place.

12. Fold the cuff up and press. You may want to tack the cuff down at the underarm seam line (Figure 8).

    You're finished!

Figure 5

Figure 6

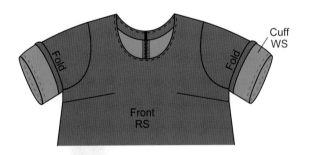

Figure 7

Figure 8

pool Tote

The Pool Tote is essential to any pool-goer's wardrobe. It's roomy enough for towels, flip-flops, a change of clothes, sunscreen, and more. It has a fun water-resistant outside pocket to protect your cell phone, keys, and other necessities that need to stay dry. Sew it in your favorite heavier weight fabric for a long-lasting poolside companion.

FABRIC

Type

For the main fabric, choose a heavyweight fabric such as canvas, denim, duck cloth, or twill.

For the lining fabric, choose a light to medium-weight woven fabric.

Quantity

44" (112 cm) wide:
Main, 1 1/4 yards (1.1 m);
Lining, 1 1/4 yards (1.1 m)
54" (137 cm) wide:
Main, 3/4 yard (0.7 m);
Lining, 7/8 yard (0.8 m)

OTHER MATERIALS

Heavy fusible interfacing (such as Pellon 809), 40" (101.5 cm) wide, 2 yards (1.8 m)

One-sided fusible interfacing (such as Pellon 71F Peltex), 20" (51 cm) wide, 1/2 yard (0.5 m)

Utility mesh, 1/3 yard (0.3 m)

16-gauge clear vinyl, 1/3 yard (0.3 m)

1 1/2" (3.8 cm) belting or heavy-weight trim, 2 yards (1.8 m)

1 package 1/4" (6 mm) elastic

Magnetic closure

Safety pin

Wonder clips

Zipper foot

Pool Tote pattern: 2 pieces

cutting instructions

MAIN FABRIC
Two 27" x 15" (68.5 x 38 cm) pieces for tote front and back

1 Pool Tote Bottom A pattern piece

LINING FABRIC
Two 27" x 15" (68.5 x 38 cm) pieces for tote front and back

1 Pool Tote Bottom A pattern piece

One 3" x 33" (7.5 x 84 cm) piece for casing for mesh

Two 3" x 10" (7.5 x 25.5 cm) pieces for casing for zipper pocket

HEAVY FUSIBLE INTERFACING
Four 27" x 15" (68.5 x 38 cm) pieces for tote front and back

2 Pool Tote Bottom A pieces

UTILITY MESH
One 10" x 33" (25.5 x 84 cm) piece for inner mesh pocket

16-GAUGE VINYL
One 10" x 8" (25.5 x 20.5 cm) piece for outer clear pocket

ONE-SIDED FUSIBLE INTERFACING
1 Pool Tote Bottom B pattern piece

1/4" (6 MM) ELASTIC
One 27" (68.5 cm) length

STRAPS
Two 36" (91.5 cm) strips of belting or 1 1/2" (3.8 cm) trim, or create your own straps using a coordinating or contrasting fabric (as seen here).

make your own straps

1. Cut two strips of fabric measuring 4" x 36" (10 x 91.5 cm).

2. Take one strip and fold and press it in half lengthwise with right sides together.

3. Unfold and then fold and press the two long raw edges in to the center crease.

4. Fold and press along the center crease again so the raw edges of your fabric are enclosed in the strap.

5. Topstitch along the open edge at 1/4" (6 mm) and along the folded edge at 1/4" (6 mm).

Repeat for the other strap.

pattern

1. Add the heavy fusible interfacing to the lining fabrics and main fabrics according to manucfacturer's directions.

2. Fold and press the 3" × 33" (7.5 × 84 cm) piece of lining fabricwrong sides together with the long sides matching. Unfold and refold the long edges toward the center fold; fold in half again. Press in place (Figure 1).

3. Sandwich the top of the mesh casing in between the fold and topstitch 1/4" (6 mm) away from the edge. Attach a safety pin to one end of the elastic, insert it into the casing with the mesh, and shimmy it all the way through. Stitch the edges down on each side (Figure 2).

4. Using a basting stitch, gather along the other long edge of the mesh.

5. Align the utility mesh to the center and bottom of one of your front or back lining pieces. Stitch it in place along both sides and across the bottom at 3/8" (1 cm). Stitch down the center of the mesh pocket to create two pockets and set the unit aside with the other lining piece (Figure 3).

6. Repeat Step 2 for the two 3" × 10" (7.5 × 25.5 cm) pieces.

7. Sandwich the top of the vinyl between the fold of one casing and topstitch 1/4" (6 mm) away from the edge. Using the other folded piece, sandwich the top of your zipper and topstitch 1/4" (6 mm) away from the edge using the zipper foot. Align the top of the vinyl covered with the fabric on the bottom portion of the zipper and stitch it in place close to the zipper teeth.

8. Cut off any excess zipper from the edges, but be sure the zipper pull is in the center, so you don't cut that off as well. Align and center the vinyl piece with the attached zipper to the bottom center of your main fabric. Hold it in place using Wonder clips. Stitch across the top edge and baste around the three remaining edges at 1/4" (6 mm) (Figure 4).

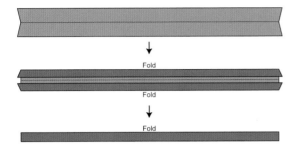

Figure 1

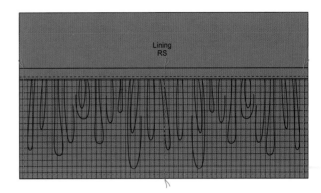

Figure 3

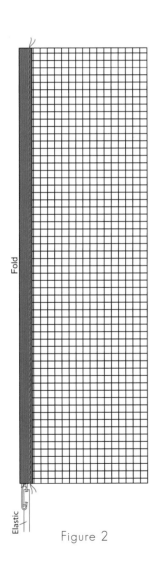

Figure 4

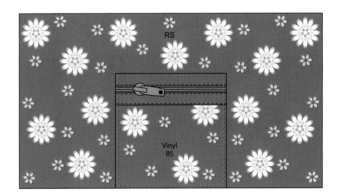

Figure 2

9. Measure from one side edge 7½" (19 cm) and pin one side of your strap, matching its raw edges with the bottom of the bag and enclosing the pocket. Repeat the same on the other side. Stitch it in place along both long edges, stopping 3" (7.5 cm) from the top of the main fabric. Repeat this for the other strap and the other piece of main fabric (Figure 5).

10. Place your two lining pieces right sides together. Sew along the side seams at ½" (1.3 cm). Repeat this for your main pieces.

11. With right sides facing and lining up the side seams with the centers of the bottom ends, attach the bottom lining piece to the main lining piece at ½" (1.3 cm). Repeat this for the main piece (Figure 6).

12. Take the bag lining and find the center top on both sides of the bag. Measure down 1½" (3.8 cm) and mark the places for the magnetic closure. Insert your magnetic closure per the manufacturer's instructions.

13. Press ½" (1.3 cm) toward the wrong side on both the bag lining and the bag main unit along the top edge. The bag front should be right side out, and the bag lining should be wrong side out (Figure 7).

14. Place the bag lining inside the bag front and align the side seams. Hold the pieces in place with wonder clips. Topstitch around the top of the bag at ½" (1.3 cm) and again at ¼" (6 mm) (Figure 8).

Now head to the pool!

7 ½"   7 ½"

Figure 5

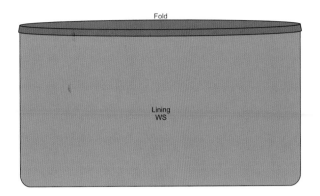

Fold

Lining
WS

Figure 7

Lining
Bottom
WS

Figure 6

Figure 8

uptown crossbody bag

Before having a child, I didn't realize how amazing it was to leave the house with a single bag for my wallet, keys, cell phone, and lipstick. No diapers, wipes, toys, snacks, bottles ... oh! Did I grab a change of clothes?! The Uptown Crossbody Bag is a great purse to use when you're not in "mom mode"—it's simple, small (but not too small), and spacious enough to fit the essentials. PLUS, it can be worn hands-free!

FABRIC

Type

For the main fabric, choose a heavyweight fabric such as canvas, denim, duck cloth, or twill.

For the lining fabric, choose a light to medium-weight woven fabric.

Quantity

44" (112 cm) wide:
Main, 1/2 yard (0.5 m);
Lining, 1/2 yard (0.5 m)

54" (137 cm) wide:
Main, 1/2 yard (0.5 m);
Lining, 1/2 yard (0.5 m)

OTHER MATERIALS

Heavy fusibile interfacing (such as Pellon 809), 40" (101.5 cm) wide, 1 1/2 yards (1.4 m)

1 adjustable shoulder strap with swivel hooks

1 magnetic snap set

Two 1/2" (1.3 cm) D rings

Wonder clips
Uptown Crossbody Bag pattern:
1 piece

cutting instructions

MAIN FABRIC

One 12¼" × 16" (31 × 40.5 cm) piece for bag front

One 2½" × 16" (6.5 × 40.5 cm) piece for top of bag back

One 10½" × 16" (26.5 × 40.5 cm) piece for bottom of bag back

Two 2" × 3" (5 × 7.5 cm) pieces for D-ring loops

1 Uptown Crossbody Bag pattern piece

LINING FABRIC

Two 12¼" × 16" (31 × 40.5 cm) pieces for bag lining

1 Uptown Crossbody Bag pattern piece

FUSIBLE INTERFACING

One 12¼" × 16" (31 × 40.5 cm) piece

One 2½" × 16" (6.5 × 40.5 cm) piece

One 10½" × 16" (26.5 × 40.5 cm) piece

2 Uptown Crossbody Bag pattern pieces

pattern

1. Iron the interfacing to the main fabrics.

2. Per the manufacturer's instructions, insert the male piece of the magnetic snap on the designated place on the flap lining.

3. Lay the lining flap piece right-side up and align the main flap piece right side down, matching the four edges. Pin and sew in place around three edges, leaving the top open for turning.

4. Snip the curved edges of the flap piece to within a few threads of the seam and turn to the right side. Press the edges really well so they have a neat finish (Figure 1).

5. Lay the bottom back piece right side up, the flap piece right side up, and the top back piece wrong side up, aligning all three pieces along the top edge. Pin and stitch the top edge in place (Figure 2).

6. Press the seam allowance toward the bottom and topstitch in place at ¼" (6 mm).

7. Align the assembled bag back piece with the front piece along the two side edges and bottom edge. Pin and stitch them in place along these three sides.

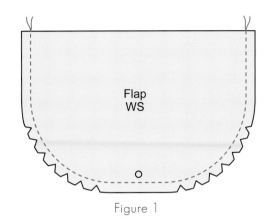

Figure 1

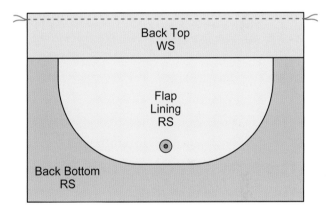

Figure 2

8. Create a gusset by pinching the corner of the bag and aligning the side seam with the bottom seam. Stitch a straight line parallel to 1" (2.5 cm) from the corner. Repeat for the other corner. Trim the seam allowances to 1/4" (6 mm) (Figure 3).

9. Place the lining pieces right sides together and stitch along the bottom and two sides. Repeat Step 8 for the lining to create the same width gusset (Figure 4).

10. Per the manufacturer's instructions, insert the female piece of the magnetic snap on the designated place on the main flap.

11. Prepare your D-ring fabric pieces by pressing the 3" (7.5 cm) sides toward the wrong side at 1/2" (1.3 cm). Press again so the raw edges are enclosed, and topstitch in place. Thread one fabric loop through a D ring and baste the ends together.

12. Press 1/2" (1.3 cm) toward the wrong side on both the bag lining and the bag main fabric along the top edge. The bag front should be right-side out and the bag lining should have the wrong side facing the wrong side of the bag fabric.

13. Place the bag lining inside the bag front and align the side seams. Hold them in place with Wonder clips. At each of the side seams, insert the raw edges of one of the D-ring loops 1/2" (1.3 cm). Topstitch around the top of the bag at 1/4" (6 mm) making sure to secure the D-ring loops at each of the side seams (Figure 5).

14. Clip your leather straps to the D rings and enjoy your Uptown Crossbody Tote (Figure 6).

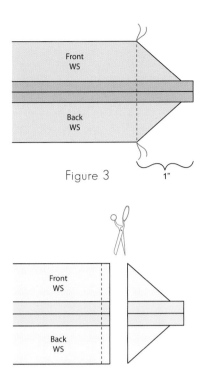

Figure 3

Figure 4

Figure 5

Figure 6

traveler's tote/backpack

The Traveler's Tote/Backpack is an incredibly versatile bag that can be worn across the body, as a shoulder purse, or as a backpack. The inside is spacious and features a recessed zipper, and the front showcases a small pocket for keeping essentials.

FABRIC

Type

For the main fabric, choose a heavyweight fabric such as canvas, denim, duck cloth, or twill.

For the lining fabric, choose a light to medium-weight woven fabric.

Quantity

44" (112 cm) wide:
Main, 1 1/4 yards (1.2 m);
Lining, 1 1/8 yards (1 m)

54" (137 cm) wide:
Main, 1 1/4 yards (1 m);
Lining, 7/8 yard (0.8 m)

OTHER MATERIALS

Heavy fusible interfacing (such as Pellon 809), 40" (101.5 cm) wide, 1 1/2 yards (1.4 m)

One-sided fusible interfacing (such as Pellon 71F Peltex), 20" (51 cm) wide, 1/4 yard (0.2 m)

1 adjustable shoulder strap with swivel hooks

One 20" (51 cm) zipper

1 magnetic snap set

Five 1/2" (1.3 cm) D rings

Safety pin

Traveler's Tote/Backpack pattern: 1 piece

cutting instructions

MAIN FABRIC

Two 11" × 23" (28 × 58.5 cm) pieces for bottom of bag, front and back

Two 4" × 23" (10 × 58.5 cm) pieces for top of bag, front and back

Two 17½" × 3" (44.5 × 7.5 cm) pieces for zipper casing

Two 3" × 3" (7.5 × 7.5 cm) pieces for zipper tabs

Three 2" × 3" (5 × 7.5 cm) pieces for D-ring loops

Two 2½" × 12" (6.5 × 30.5 cm) pieces for bottom D-ring loops

One 7" × 16" (18 × 40.5 cm) piece for front pocket

1 Traveler's Tote/Backpack pattern piece

LINING

Two 11" × 23" (28 × 58.5 cm) pieces for bottom of bag, front and back

Two 4" × 23" (10 × 58.5 cm) pieces for top of bag, front and back

One 7" × 16" (18 × 40.5 cm) piece for front pocket

1 Traveler's Tote/Backpack pattern piece

HEAVY FUSIBLE INTERFACING

Two 11" × 23" (28 × 58.5 cm) pieces

Two 4" × 23" (10 × 58.5 cm) pieces

Two 17½" × 1½" (44.5 × 3.8 cm) pieces

1 Traveler's Tote/Backpack pattern piece

ONE-SIDED FUSIBLE INTERFACING

One 4½" × 16½" (11.5 × 42 cm) piece

pattern

1. Add heavy interfacing to the main fabrics. For the two 17 1/2" × 3" (44.5 × 7.5 cm) pieces, add interfacing to one long edge only.

2. Fold the three 2" × 3" (5 × 7.5 cm) and the two 2 1/2" × 12" (6.5 × 30.5 cm) main fabric strips in half lengthwise with right sides together. Sew along the long edges using 1/4" (6 mm) seam allowances (Figure 1). Press. For each piece, attach a safety pin to the edge of one end and use it to turn the piece right side out. Press and set aside.

3. Fold two edges of each 3" × 3" (7.5 × 7.5 cm) square with wrong sides together toward the center at 1/2" (1.3 cm) (Figure 2), then fold the other two edges toward the center at 1/2" (1.3 cm) (Figure 3). Fold each whole square in half wrong sides together (Figure 4). Set aside for use later; these go on the zipper ends.

4. Find the horizontal center of the 7" × 16" (18 × 40.5 cm) accent piece and mark down 3" (7.5 cm) from the top edge. Insert the female portion of the magnetic snap per the manufacturer's instructions.

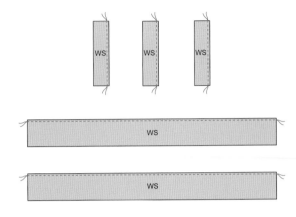

Figure 1

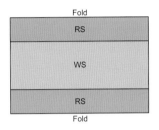

Figure 2

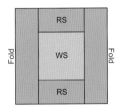

Figure 3

Figure 4

5. Place both 7" × 16" (18 × 40.5 cm) pocket pieces right sides together and sew around all four sides leaving about 2" (5 cm) unsewn for turning along the top. Flip to the right side and fold the seam allowance in toward the wrong sides on the unsewn portion. Press in place and topstitch along the top only. This is now the pocket piece.

6. Using the pattern piece as a guide, mark the place on the flap piece where the magnetic snap will go on the lining piece. Insert the male portion of the magnetic snap per the manufacturer's instructions on top of your marking.

7. Align the two flap pieces right sides together and stitch in place around three sides, leaving the top open. Clip the curved seams, turn to the right side, and press flat. This is now the pocket flap piece.

8. Lay the back main 11" × 23" (28 × 58.5 cm) piece right-side up. Take the 2½" × 12" (6.5 × 30.5 cm) strips from Step 2 (now measuring 1" × 12" [2.5 × 30.5 cm]). Fold them in half and insert a D ring into the loop. Align the two raw edges with the raw edge of the bottom of the main piece starting 4½" (11.5 cm) from each side edge. Sew the loops to the main bag back, stopping 1" (2.5 cm) from the folded edge of the loop. Stitch across the strip and down the other side (Figure 5).

9. Take one of the 2" × 3" (5 × 7.5 cm) pieces from Step 2 (now measuring ¾" × 3" [2 × 7.5 cm]) and fold it in half. Insert a D ring into the loop and baste the raw ends of the loop to the top center of the main bag back.

10. Align the two main back 4" × 23" (10 × 58.5 cm) pieces right sides together. Sew in place along the top. Press the seam up and topstitch in place. Set aside. This is now the main back piece (Figure 6).

11. Align the pocket piece in the center of the front main 11" × 23" (28 × 58.5 cm) piece 4" (10 cm) from the bottom. Edgestitch the pocket in place along the bottom and two sides.

12. Center the pocket flap right side up along the top of the 11" × 23" (28 × 58.5 cm) main front piece (Figure 7). Lay the 4" × 23" (10 × 58.5 cm) main front piece right side down on top of the pocket flap (Figure 8). Pin and stitch in place along the top edge. Press the seam up and topstitch in place. Set aside. This is now the main front piece.

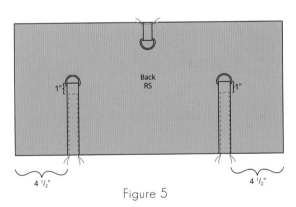

Figure 5

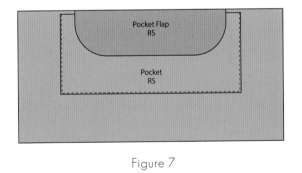

Figure 7

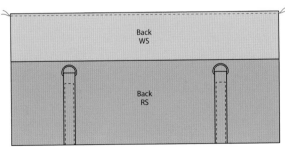

Figure 6

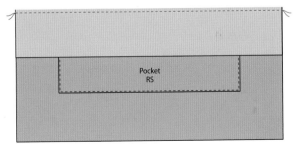

Figure 8

13. Take the two 17½" × 3" (44.5 × 7.5 cm) pieces and fold the short ends of each toward the wrong side at ¼" (6 mm) and press in place. Fold the two long edges toward the wrong side at ¼" (6 mm) and press in place (Figure 9). Fold them in half with wrong sides together so the long ends meet (Figure 10). Center the zipper tape along the folded edges, pin, and stitch in place using a zipper foot. Take the two pieces from Step 3 and place them over the ends of the zipper tape. Stitch them in place along the sandwiched ends (Figure 11).

14. Center the zipper with the right side up along the top of one of the 11" × 23" (28 × 58.5 cm) lining pieces (Figure 12). Lay the 4" × 23" (10 × 58.5 cm) lining piece right side down on top of the zipper, and front lining piece, matching raw edges. Pin and stitch in place. Repeat for the other side of the zipper and other two lining pieces. Set aside. These are now your front and back lining pieces (Figure 13).

Figure 9

Figure 10

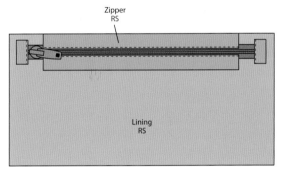

Figure 11

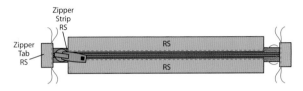

Figure 12

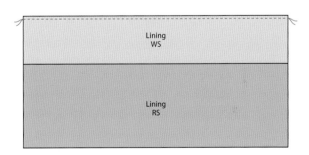

Figure 13

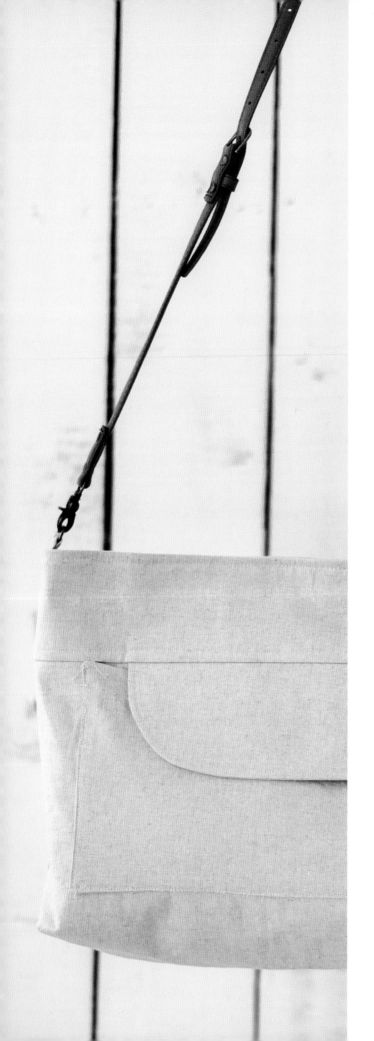

15. Align the front and back main pieces together with right sides facing. Sew along all edges but the top. Repeat for the front and back lining pieces. These will now be referred to as "bag front" and "lining."

16. Create gussets in each corner by pinching the corner of the bag and aligning the side seam with the bottom seam. Stitch a straight line parallel to 2" (5 cm) from the corner. Repeat for the other corners (bag front and lining). Trim the seam allowances to ¼" (6 mm) (Figures 14 and 15).

17. Press ½" (1.3 cm) toward the wrong side on both the lining and the bag front along the top edge. The bag front should be right-side out and the bag lining should be wrong-side out (Figure 16).

18. Using the remaining two rectangles from Step 2, thread them each through a D ring and baste the ends together.

19. Insert the one-sided fusible interfacing inside the bag front and place along the bottom. Place the bag lining inside the bag front, sandwiching the fusible and aligning the side seams. Hold in place with Wonder clips. At each of the side seams, insert the unfinished edge of one of the D-ring loops about ½" (1.3 cm). Topstitch around the top of the bag at ¼" (6 mm) making sure to secure the D-ring loops at each of the side seams (Figure 17).

20. To wear it as a tote bag, hook your adjustable strap to the two D rings at the side seams. To wear it as a backpack, hook your adjustable strap to the two D rings at the base of the bag back and through the loop at the center (Figure 18).

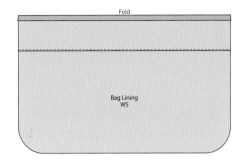

Figure 16

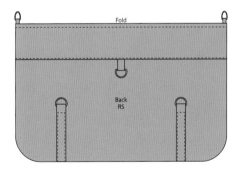

Figure 17

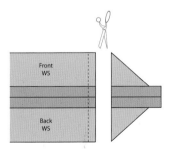

Figure 14

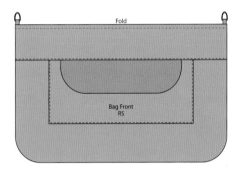

Figure 18

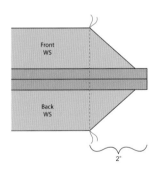

Figure 15

tie belt

This simple-to-sew belt is the perfect accessory to add to a shift dress waist or pair of shorts with loopholes (like the Boardwalk Shorts, page 60!). It's just two long strips of fabric sewn together and tied into a sweet bow or knot for a perfectly casual look.

FABRIC

Type
Woven fabric such as cotton, chambray, or Tencel

Quantity
½ yard (0.5 m)

OTHER MATERIALS
Tie Belt: 1 pattern piece

pattern

1. Fold the fabric in half lengthwise with right sides together so the long edges are aligned (Figures 1 and 2).

2. Stitch in place along the three open sides. Leave a 2" (5 cm) opening for turning in the middle of the long edge. Clip the points off the ends to within ⅛" (3 mm) of the stitching (Figure 3).

3. Pull the belt right-side out and press all the seams flat. Topstitch in place right over the opening and around the edge of the belt. Pair it with your Boardwalk Shorts!

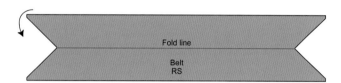

Figure 1

Figure 2

Figure 3

turban twist headband

Keep your hair out of your eyes with the stylish Turban Twist Headband. Sewn with knit fabric, it will stretch over your head and right into your hair.

FABRIC

Type
Lightweight to medium-weight stretchy fabric such as jersey knit, cotton Lycra, or rayon Lycra

Quantity
½ yard (0.3 m)

CUTTING INSTRUCTIONS
Two 6" × 28" (15 × 71 cm) strips

pattern

1. Lay the two strips in a cross style, one vertically with the right side up and one horizontally with the wrong side up (Figure 1).

2. Fold the horizontal strip in half so the two wrong sides are facing, the short raw edges are aligned, and the other strip is sandwiched in between (Figure 2).

3. Repeat Step 2 for the other strip of fabric (Figure 3).

4. Pull the short raw edges so they are even and align all four edges together and stitch them in place. Turn the turban so the seam is on the inside (Figure 4).

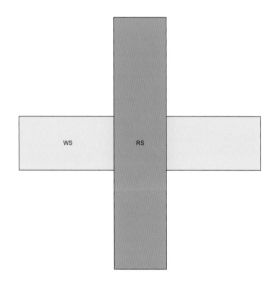

Figure 1

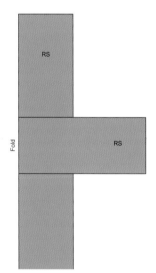

Figure 2

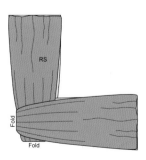

Figure 3

Figure 4

slingback flip-flops

Transform a boring pair of flip-flops into something unique with fabric I bet you already have in your stash.

FABRIC

Type

Lightweight to medium-weight stretchy fabric such as jersey knit, cotton Lycra, or rayon Lycra

Quantity

½ yard (0.5 m)

OTHER MATERIALS

1 pair flip-flops

Hot glue

Nonfabric scissors

Pair of chopsticks (or similar tool with blunt end)

Large safety pin

CUTTING INSTRUCTIONS

These cutting instructions are approximate and are based on an average women's size 8 shoe size. Adjust accordingly for your correct fit.

Two 2" × 4" (5 × 10 cm) pieces for toe dividers

Two 8" × 6" (20.5 × 15 cm) pieces for instep straps

Two 14" × 6" (35.5 × 15 cm) pieces for toe-to-heel straps

pattern

Cut the plastic straps off your flip-flops and discard them.

1. Take the small 2"x 4" (5 × 10 cm) strips and fold them in half lengthwise with right sides together. Sew along the long edge at $1/4$" (6 mm). Attach a large safety pin to one side of the end of the strip. Feed it through the strip to turn it right side out. Press. Insert the short, unsewn ends from the top into the front hole of the flip-flop. Use the chopsticks to help get the ends through the hole, leaving about $1/2$" (1.3 cm) of the loop sticking out. Using your glue gun, squeeze a generous amount of glue into the flip-flop hole. As you glue the fabric to the flip-flop, firmly press the ends into the hole. Keep gluing until the ends feel secure.

    Repeat this for the other flip-flop.

2. Take one of the 14" × 6" (35.5 × 15 cm) strips and thread it through the loop-hole you created. Align the short edges to one another with right sides facing in and stitch in place at $1/4$" (6 mm). Flip the fabric so the right side is facing out and repeat for the other flip-flop. (Note: The long edges are left raw—since you're using a knit fabric, there's no need to worry about fraying.)

3. Take one of your 8" × 6" (20.5 × 15 cm) pieces and insert one of the 6" (15 cm) sides into the left bottom hole. Repeat the gluing process found in Step 1. Take the other edge and repeat for the bottom right hole. (Note: The 8" [20.5 cm] edges are left raw).

4. Thread the longer loop of fabric under the short loop and try them on!

glossary

Backstitch—Sewing two or three stitches back and forth at the beginning and ends of stitch lines to anchor the stitches in place and keep them from coming undone.

Basting—A long stitch used to hold pieces together before actual sewing OR to gather fabric to create a ruffle or bunching of fabric.

Bias—The stretchiest part of the fabric that runs diagonally (at a 45-degree angle) to the grainline of the fabric.

Crossgrain—The direction of the fabric that runs perpendicular to the selvedge.

Edgestitch—To stitch as closely to the raw or folded edge as possible.

Finger Press—To open a seam allowance or make a slight crease on fabric using only your finger or thumb.

Grainline—The direction of the fabric that runs parallel to the selvedge.

Interfacing—Used to stabilize fabrics. Lighter weight interfacing is used in clothing for things such as waistbands and buttonholes. Heavier weight interfacing is used in bags to make them stand and withhold wear and tear.

Overlock Stitch—Used to "lock" the raw edge in place. A serger easily creates an overlock stitch, but a regular sewing machine has this capability as well!

Right Side (RS, or sometimes RST [right sides together])—This is the printed, "pretty" side of the fabric. With some fabrics it is obvious which is the "right" and "wrong" side of the fabric. Others are not so obvious, and some may not technically have a "right" or a "wrong" side. A good tip for determining the "right" side is to hold two opposite sides of the fabric into natural light and figure out which looks best, has the most color saturation, etc.

Seam Allowance (SA)—The area between the stitch line and the raw edge of fabric. For the patterns in this book, seam allowance is $1/2$" (1.3 cm), unless otherwise noted.

Selvedge—The edge of the fabric that is marked with the manufacturer's and/or designer's information as well as a color chart.

Stitch in the Ditch—This term refers to the "ditch" created by a seam that is shown on the right side of the fabric opposite the seam allowance. When you "stitch in the ditch," your stitches disappear into the "ditch." This is a great technique to use for attaching a waistband lining to the wrong side of your skirt.

Topstitch—Used to add stability to seam allowances along areas such as necklines and hems, these stitches will be seen when wearing your garment, so be sure to choose your thread accordingly!

Wrong Side (WS, or sometimes WST [wrong sides together])—The unprinted side of the fabric. See "Right Side" for tips on differentiating the two.

Metric Conversion Chart		
To Convert	**To**	**Multiply By**
Inches	Centimeters	2.54
Centimeters	Inches	0.4
Feet	Centimeters	30.5
Centimeters	Feet	0.03
Yards	Meters	0.9
Meters	Yards	1.1

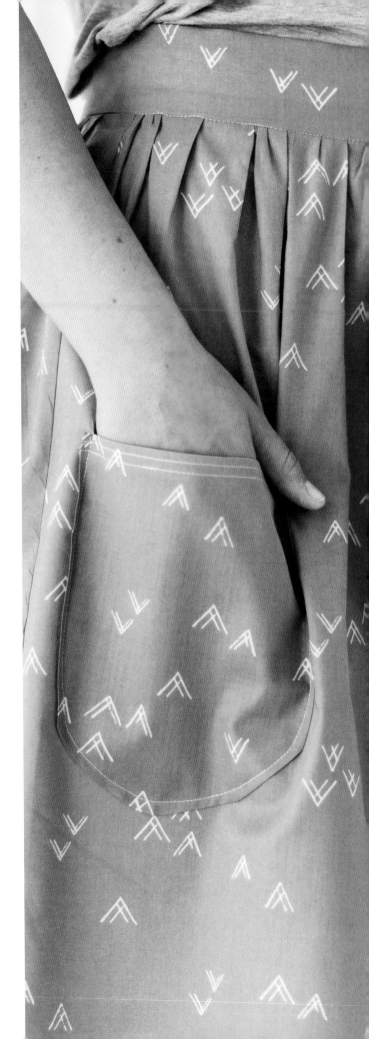

fabrics used in this book

AFTERNOON SKIRT
(green skirt) cotton voile, Wanderer from Art Gallery Fabrics

(gray top) Tilly Tee, rayon spandex blend

BOARDWALK SHORTS
(blue shorts) Tencel

(belt) Tie Belt, Tencel

(floral top) Tilly Tee, knit, Paperie from Art Gallery Fabrics

(bag) Uptown Crossbody Bag, Frosted Sage Denim from Art Gallery Fabrics

BUTTON-UP TANK
(yellow top) cotton in honey, Art Gallery Pure Element

(floral shorts) Boardwalk Shorts, cotton, Millie Fleur from Art Gallery Fabrics

COLONIAL COVER-UP
knit, Happy Home Fabrics from Art Gallery Fabrics

DARLING SHIFT DRESS
Ikat Rayon Challis

DATE NIGHT SKIRT
(floral skirt) cotton, Chalk and Paint from Art Gallery Fabrics

(pink top) Tilly Tee, Art Gallery Knit in Crystal Pink

sequin mesh knit, lined with cotton

LARCHMONT TEE
cotton voile, Fantasia from Art Gallery Fabrics

POOL TOTE
cotton canvas, Sketchbook from Art Gallery Fabrics

SATURDAY MORNING SHORTS
cotton, Dare from Art Gallery Fabrics

TILLY TEE
knit, Lavis from Art Gallery Fabrics

TRAVELER'S TOTE/BACKPACK
linen blend cotton, Art Gallery Fabrics

UPTOWN CROSSBODY BAG
woven chambray, Robert Kaufman

TURBAN TWIST
Art Gallery knit solid

FLIP FLOPS
knit, Chalk and Paint from Art Gallery

index

dedication

To my daughter, Tinsley, who was born in the middle of this crazy writing process. I hope one day you grow up and chase all of your dreams.

acknowledgements

Writing a book is no easy task—it really and truly takes a village. I am so fortunate to have friends and family who support my business and all of my wild ideas.

To my husband, David: Your support and encouragement over the years is something I will always cherish; you always help me dream big and to never settle. Thanks for being there and for supporting me in every aspect of life. I love you!

To my mom, Scarlett: Thank you for being my biggest cheerleader, for helping watch Tinsley so I could write this book, and for always being willing to drop everything to help me at a moment's notice. I thank the Lord every day that you are my mom!

To my mother-in-law, Mitzi: Thank you for your love and support, your selflessness, and your willingness to watch Tinsley during the months of writing. I can't thank you enough!

To the rest of our family (Dad, Al, Joanna, Jonny, Rachael, and Andrew): Thank you from the bottom of my heart for your love, encouragement, and support. I hope I've made you proud. I love you guys!

To my (incredible) photographer, Sarah: I LOVE YOU. I can't say it enough. You can somehow get inside my head and make my thoughts reality. You are one of a kind, and I am so happy the Lord brought us together. It's such an honor and blessing to call you a friend and colleague.

To my small group at church (Audrey, Brandon, Katie, Travis, Lauren, Cole, Marissa, Brad, Kelly, and Dave): You are my people, and I'm so thrilled I get to walk through life with you. Thank you for your prayers through this writing process and for always being such an encouragement to me in my business.

To my sewing besties, Erin and Kristen: Thanks for always being one text away; I am so thankful for your friendship!

To my loyal online friends/followers/fans: YOU GUYS ARE THE BEST! I would not be where I am today if it had not been for your support and encouragement. Thank you for being my inspiration—I can't wait to see what you create using this book!

Finally, thanks to God, for His grace upon grace and unending faithfulness.

ABOUT THE AUTHOR

Caroline Hulse is the author and designer behind the brand Sew Caroline. She is a sewing blogger with a serious passion for handmade fashion, a sewing-pattern designer who creates trendy, easy-to-sew patterns for women, and a licensed fabric designer for Art Gallery Fabrics. Her work has been featured in numerous print publications such as *Stitch*, *Love Patchwork & Quilting*, *Quilts and More*, *Sew It All*, and *Sew Style & Home*. She has appeared on Sew It All TV and It's Sew Easy TV, and she has a few online classes available through Craft Daily.

In her work Caroline strives to create an uplifting and creative atmosphere that inspires people to create something new—and keep coming back for more. Caroline resides in Fort Worth, Texas, with her husband, David, their daughter, Tinsley, and their fur baby, Sammie.

Find Caroline online:

Website: www.sewcaroline.com

Shop: www.shopsewcaroline.com

Instagram: @sewcaroline

what will you sew next?

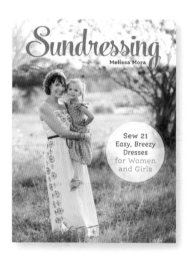

SUNDRESSING:
SEW 21 EASY, BREEZY DRESSES FOR WOMEN AND GIRLS

by Melissa Mora

Create 21 fun, feminine looks that capture the essence of summer!

ISBN: 978-1-44024-454-4
Price: $26.99

SIGNATURE BAGS:
12 TREND-SETTING BAG PATTERNS TO SEW AT HOME

by Michelle Golightly

In this fashion-forward collection, you'll find clutches, totes, and purses that will suit any occasion and complement any look.

ISBN: 978-1-44024-420-9
Price: $ 24.99

Y:
EW MAKE

s never

features dozens ot beginner-friendly projects with professional polish.

ISBN: 978-1-44024-560-2
Price: $24.99

Fons&Porter

Available at your favorite retailer or the Fons & Porter store.
shopfonsandporter.com